CW01638722

# Clifton Park

## THE JEWEL IN ROTHERHAM'S CROWN
## 1891 - 2015

Elaine Humphries

Published by Elaine Humphries

All rights reserved
Copyright ©Elaine Humphries 2015

Printed by B&B Press (Parkgate) Ltd
Rotherham

I dedicate this book to my family, Gerald, Jane and Baz, Jill and my special grandsons Ryan and Jack.

## FOREWORD

I have lived in the Clifton area of Rotherham most of my life and have visited Clifton Park regularly from being a small child.

I have seen many changes as a child, parent and now grandparent, and I still appreciate its beauty during every season.

Many articles have been written over the years about the Park and the Walker Family, I have brought most of these together to give the history of the Park from it's opening in 1891 and how it has evolved over its 124 years.

I hope my book brings back memories of Clifton Park to everyone who reads it, and the many people who have used the park, either for pleasure or during their working life.

My very special thanks go to all the staff at Rotherham Archives and Local Studies for their help, not forgetting the many people who have shared their stories with me. A big thank you to Emily Green for the word-processing and to Pippa Harder for her help.

Elaine Humphries 2015

# INDEX

## CLIFTON PARK.

IN 1860 CAME A REMARK,
"ROTHERHAM CITIZENS HAVE NO PARK."
"WHY NOT CLIFTON PARK ?" THEY SAID.
"AFTER ALL, - OLD WALKER'S DEAD."

IN 1883, AGAIN WAS THOUGHT,
THAT CLIFTON PARK SHOULD NOW BE BOUGHT.
"HERE'S MY FEW POUNDS" THE WRITER STATES,
"GET THE REST FROM THE LOCAL RATES".

AGAIN TO BUY WAS THE PERSISTENT THEME
"CLIFTON PARK FOR THE PUBLIC" SCHEME
AND 1887 IT SEEMS
WAS NOT THE YEAR FOR ATTAINING DREAMS.

£18,000 IS OFFERED, AND REFUSED,
THAT MIGHTY SUM WAS QUITE ABUSED
THE MAYOR IS DETERMINED TO HAVE HIS WAY
AND £25,000 WINS THE DAY.

COME OUT TO PLAY, SHOUT, DANCE AND SING,
FROM LONDON TOWN HAS COME THE KING,
HE'S COME TO OPEN CLIFTON PARK.
ALDERMAN NEILL, YOU'VE MADE YOUR MARK

DAYS HAVE PASSED, YEARS HAVE FLOWN
WE STILL HAVE CLIFTON PARK TO CALL OUR OWN
AT FIRST THEY COULD ONLY WALK OR SIT
BUT GREAT IMPROVEMENTS, CAME BIT BY BIT.

GILBERT AND SULLIVAN FOR MUSIC LOVERS,
CUPS OF TEA FOR HARASSED MOTHERS,
PADDLING POOL, SANDS AND SLIDES,
TENNIS, BOWLS AND DONKEY RIDES.

HORSE JUMPING AT ROTHERHAM SHOW
ON AND ON, AND ON, WE GO
IS IT ALL FOR PLEASURE ?
NO !!!

OUR CENOTAPH HAS PRIDE OF PLACE
WITHIN ITS GATES - IT'S NO DISGRACE.
OUR ROTHERHAM MEN - YOUR CENOTAPH
IN CLIFTON PARK - YOUR EPITAPH.

DOREEN HADLEY 1988.

# 1 THE CLIFTON ESTATE

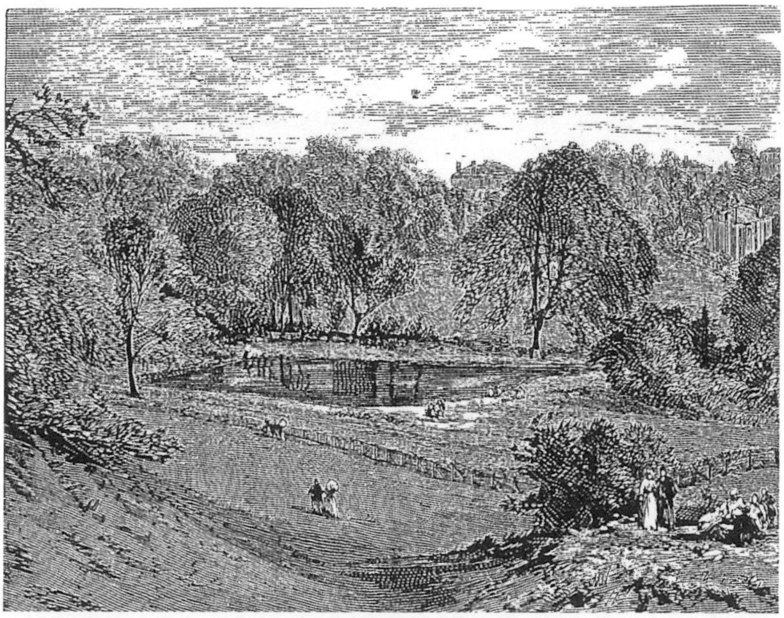

*London Illustrated News. This is perhaps one of the first photo's of the lake, June 27th 1891. (Rotherham Archives)*

The earliest detailed information of ownership of the Land now called Clifton Park is to be found in the Rotherham Enclosure Award of 1764, it was listed in 1746 as belonging to the Earl of Effingham.

It originally formed part of a large open field known as Gallowtree Hill Field or Haslegreave, consisting of about 193 acres. The Gallow Tree or Gibbet stood near the site of the present Clifton Hotel on Clifton Lane.

Private and Public roads surrounded the field and the same roads are now very busy roads:

- The Turnpike Road for Tinsley to Doncaster became Doncaster Road
- Woodhouse Leys Road became Badsley Moor Lane
- Gallowtree Hill Road became Clifton Lane
- Castleforthsike Road became Far Lane
- A private road called Eldertree Road, which ran through the middle of the field from Doncaster Road to Woodhouse Leys Road, became Middle Lane
- Eastwood Road, called Birdcage Lane in 1851, became St Ann's Road.

Samuel Walker is listed as subscribing 10 Guineas to the new Tinsley and Doncaster Turnpike road. An early shareholder!

Joshua Walker bought part of this large field, on it he built his house and surrounded the entire estate with a stone wall. He and his wife, Susannah, moved into Clifton House in 1783.

Joshua may not have been the first to take up residence, as there is evidence of an Iron Age settlement nearby on this elevated site.

The Parish of Clifton was not created until 1887, so it may have been called after the Clifton Estate. The OS map reference is SK 435930.

The earliest record of a 'park' is in a survey drawing of 1820, five years after Joshua Walker's death. It records features which include two walled gardens, pleasure grounds, drives, walls, fences, gateways, individual trees and a fishpond; but the 'pleasure grounds' covered only half of the estate, the remainder being divided by a ha-ha or retaining wall. It was hidden from the house below ground level with a ditch that prevented stock from wandering into the pleasure gardens and eating the plants.

The grandest entrance to the Walker Estate seemed to be on the North-West of the house (halfway up Clifton Lane). The perimeter walls curved to pillars set back from the carriageway allowing access to the main west front of the house. Other narrower drives lead to smaller gates on Doncaster Road.

Henry and Elizabeth Walker, Joshua's son and wife, enlarged the parkland, changing the entrances, building Birdcage Lodge and redecorating the house.
Elizabeth Walker died in 1850 and Henry in January 1860. By May 1860, the 69-acre estate was up for sale, divided into 9 lots. A local iron and steel manufacturer, William Owen Esq of Phoenix Iron Works, purchased the house and land in 1864.
Suggestions by Rotherham Corporation about buying the estate for the town first surfaced at this time and were noted in the newspapers of the day.

In 1875, Rotherham Corporation laid a sewer through the park to drain the district adjoining Badsley Moor Lane; it is shown on early maps passing through the park towards Doncaster Road and on the plans of 1883 relating to the sale. William Owen attempted to claim compensation from the Council for the laying of the sewer, but failed.

Owen built two cottages inside the estate near the Clifton Grove entrance for his employees. The 1881 Census shows that the Head Gardener, John Stevenson, and Head Coachman Henry Frost occupied them.

William Owen died in 1881 and his wife, Catherine, shortly after in 1882. A tenant, Charles H Thornhill Esq, occupied the house before the estate was placed back on the market in February 1883.

Rotherham Corporation purchased Clifton House and the Estate for £25,000 in 1891 then proceeded to convert it into Rotherham's second public park. Two years later Clifton House opened as a museum.

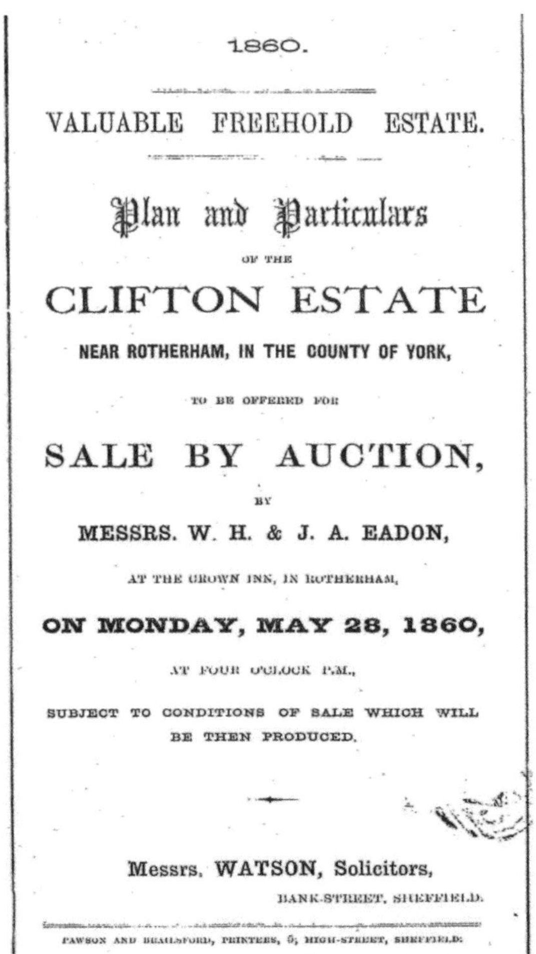
1860.

VALUABLE FREEHOLD ESTATE.

Plan and Particulars

OF THE

CLIFTON ESTATE

NEAR ROTHERHAM, IN THE COUNTY OF YORK,

TO BE OFFERED FOR

SALE BY AUCTION,

BY

MESSRS. W. H. & J. A. EADON,

AT THE CROWN INN, IN ROTHERHAM,

ON MONDAY, MAY 28, 1860,

AT FOUR O'CLOCK P.M.,

SUBJECT TO CONDITIONS OF SALE WHICH WILL BE THEN PRODUCED.

Messrs. WATSON, Solicitors,

BANK-STREET, SHEFFIELD.

PAWSON AND BRAILSFORD, PRINTERS, 5, HIGH-STREET, SHEFFIELD.

In July 1891, an order was given to the Mayor of Rotherham to purchase the two cottages. A male urinal was built behind these cottages in 1892; the hexagonal roof, which was part of it, can still be seen. In 1913, a privet hedge was planted around the cottages to separate them from the park.

# VALUABLE FREEHOLD ESTATE.

# THE CLIFTON ESTATE,

**NEAR ROTHERHAM, IN THE COUNTY OF YORK,**

WILL BE OFFERED FOR

# SALE BY AUCTION,

BY

## MESSRS. W. H. AND J. A. EADON,

**AT THE CROWN INN, IN ROTHERHAM,**

**ON MONDAY, THE 28th DAY OF MAY, 1860,**

**AT FOUR O'CLOCK P.M.,**

**SUBJECT TO CONDITIONS OF SALE WHICH WILL BE THEN PRODUCED.**

**he whole of the Estate will firstly be offered in one Lot, and should it not be so Sold, then following or such other Lots as shall be arranged at the Sale :—**

| | A. | R. | P. |
|---|---|---|---|
| —MANSION HOUSE, with the Out-Offices, Stables, Carriage-House, Vineries, Pleasure Gardens, Fruit Gardens, Plantations, Park, Fish Pond, and Lodge | 30 | 2 | 0 |
| .—The FAR LAWN and PLANTATIONS in the occupation of Mr. John Hobson | 19 | 0 | 18 |
| .—The NEAR WELLGATE CLOSE, in the occupation of Mr. John Moorhouse | 3 | 2 | 30 |
| .—The MIDDLE BADDESLEY CLOSE and PLANTATION, in the occupation of Mr. Thomas Gillatt | 3 | 0 | 12 |
| .—The FAR BADDESLEY CLOSE and PLANTATION, in the occupation of Mr. Thomas Gillatt | 2 | 2 | 7 |
| .—CLIFTON LANE FIELD, in the occupation of Mr. Rising | 2 | 2 | 26 |
| '.—The HAYSTACK FIELD, in the occupation of Mr. Rising | 1 | 2 | 12 |
| ?.—The FAR WELLGATE CLOSE, part in the occupation of Mr. Rising and part of Mr. Moorhouse | 3 | 0 | 35 |
| ).—The PINFOLD CLOSE, in the occupation of Mr. Rising | 2 | 2 | 20 |
| | 69 | 0 | 0 |

VALUABLE FREEHOLD ESTATE.

THE

CLIFTON PARK ESTATE,

ROTHERHAM,

AND VALUABLE

BUILDING LAND

Near thereto, part of the Estates of the late WILLIAM OWEN, Esq., Deceased, will be Offered for

Sale by Auction,

BY

MESSRS. STYRING & TURNER,

AT THEIR MART, MOORGATE STREET, ROTHERHAM,

On MONDAY, the 2nd day of JULY, 1883,

Three for Four o'Clock in the Afternoon, subject to the General Conditions of Sale of the Sheffield District Incorporated Law Society, and such Special Conditions as shall be then and there produced.

Particulars and Plans and further information, also Cards to View the House and Park, may be obtained from Messrs. R. MACKAY & Co., Chartered Accountants, 8, Lothbury, London, E.C.; Mr. G. D. OWEN (Owen & Dyson), Mr. H. L. TACON, Architect and Surveyor, and the AUCTIONEERS, Rotherham; Messrs. WATSON, ESAM, & BARBER, Solicitors, Sheffield; Mr. G. M. SAUNDERS, Solicitor, Carlton Chambers, 8, Regent street, London, W.; and from

Messrs. NICHOLSON, SAUNDERS, NICHOLSON & REEDER,

... UPON DEARNE, ROTHERHAM.

Interestingly, four years before this time, the Corporation had refused to give £18,500 for the estate and house, also attempting to buy back land that had been previously sold. They purchased from a Mr Drabble and Mr Rhodes, the fishpond and adjacent plots for £2,500, but nothing could be done about the new house called 'Park Lea' that was already occupied by Mr William Cooper.

## Plan of Clifton Estate

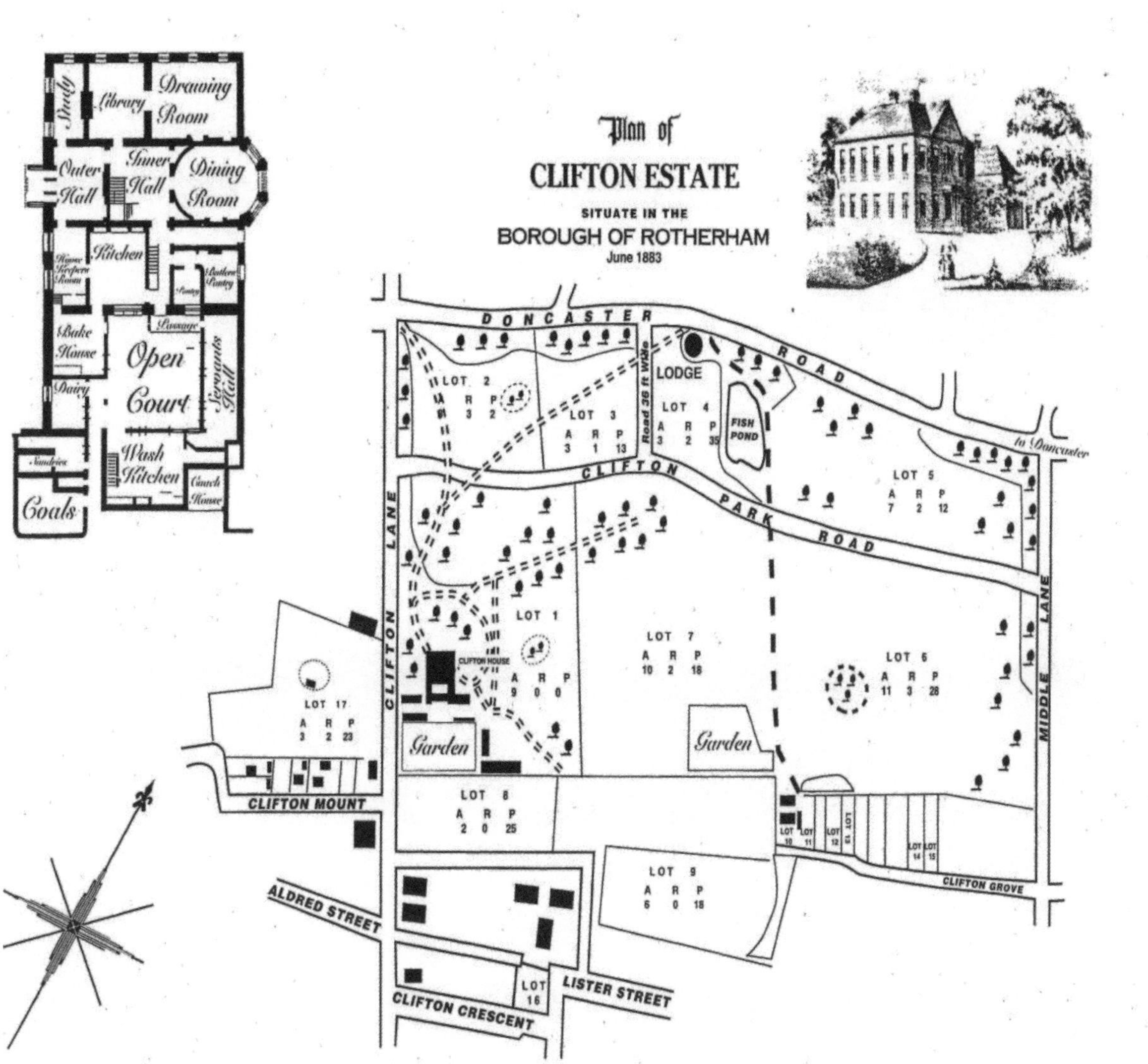


*Plan redrawn from original auction sale catalogue 1883. Scale approximately 1:6,300*

*(Rotherham Archives)*

**In the early 1900s, the Inland Revenue valued Clifton Park at £22, 825.**

## 2 CLIFTON PARK

Queen Victoria granted the Charter of Incorporation to Rotherham on 29 August 1871. However, the townspeople never saw the splendour of the Mayoral robes and Insignia of office until 25 June 1891. It was in this year that the then Prince and Princess of Wales (later to be crowned King Edward VII and Queen Alexandra) and accompanied by Princesses Maud and Victoria opened Clifton Park.

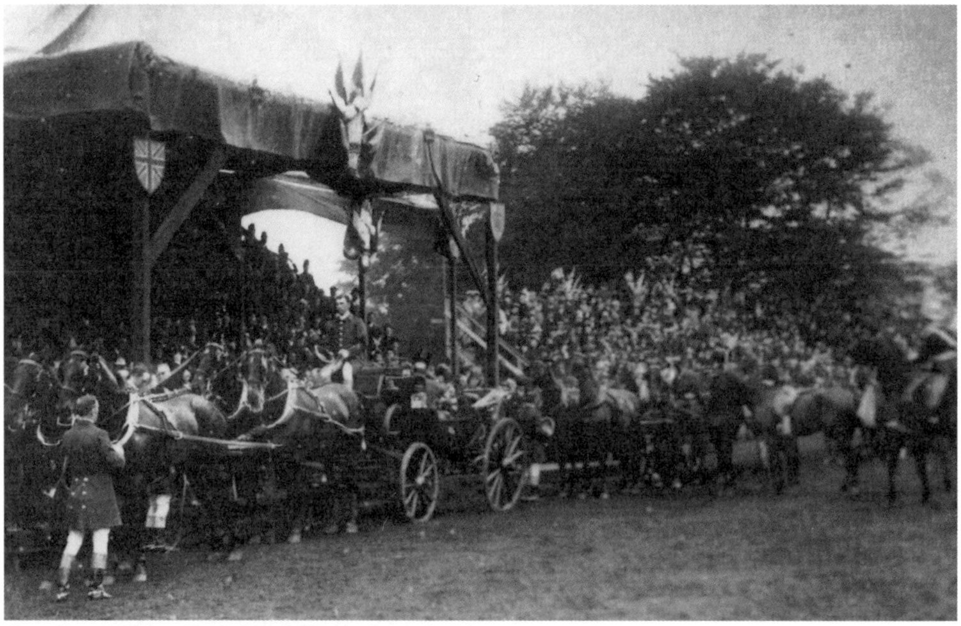

*Opening of Clifton Park 1891. (Rotherham Archives)*

The Mayor must have made a great impression, driving ahead of the Royal carriage, greeted with loud cheers. On his arrival at Clifton Park, he was accorded a perfect oration where children commenced singing, 'God Bless the Prince of Wales'.

The Feoffees of the Common Lands of Rotherham donated £25.00 to the reception fund for the Prince and Princess of Wales for the opening of Clifton Park.

Once the park had been formally opened, vast crowds went in to enjoy themselves, there being 'Festivities of many kinds' to entertain them.

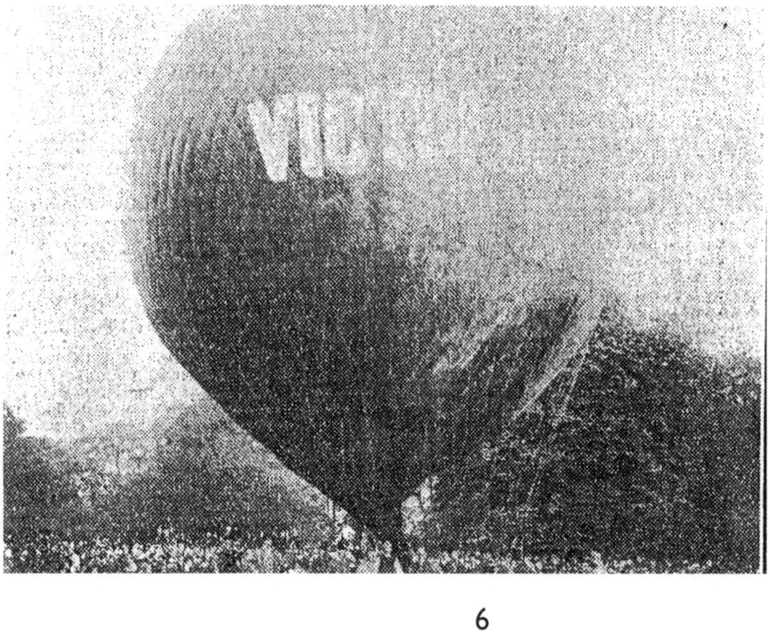

*Balloon ascent and opening of CLlifton Park. June 25th 1891. (Rotherham Archives)*

The principle attraction was a balloon ascent; it had been filled with gas from the town mains. At the start of the ascent, Councillor T. Charles had a narrow escape as, *'his legs became entangled with the rope as the balloon lifted into the air. The consequences of which would of course have been that he would have carried into the air hanging head downwards'.* Fortunately, someone noticed his predicament and he managed to free himself before the balloon sped on its journey skywards over the town towards Thorpe Hesley. The balloon the occupants of the balloon car finally landed in the middle of the moors about nine miles from Huddersfield.

In the evening, the whole affair was rounded off by a grand firework display, which included a portrait of the Mayor and the Mayoress, the Borough Coat of Arms and a naval battle.

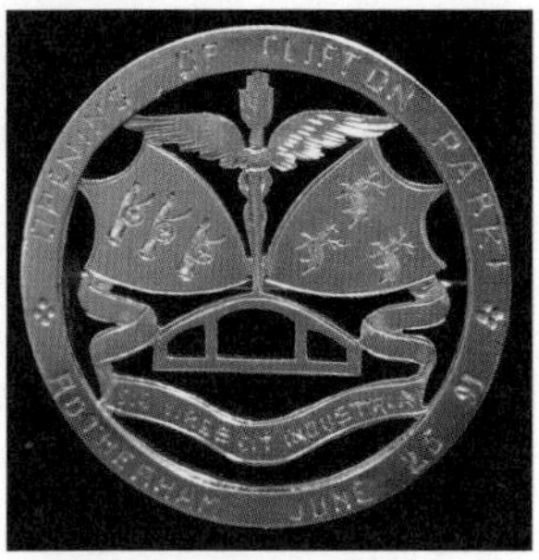
*Badge of Park opening*

A silver badge was designed and presented to local dignitaries to mark the opening of the park. (David Clark)

Quote from Rotherham Directory 1902:

*'The park is a finely timbered piece of land about 56 acres on the south side of Doncaster Road and was opened on 25 June 1891 by His Majesty Edward VII, The Prince of Wales. The corporation have enlarged the lake and laid out grounds at a cost of about £5,000.'*

Following the opening of the park, many outbuildings were removed, which suggests that the Council did not consider it fitting to have kitchen gardens and stables within a park!

The Illustrated London News ran an article in June 1891 about Clifton Park which referred to the new park and its 'noble forest trees – Beech, Oak, Elm, Horse Chestnut, Sycamore and other' and clumps of Yew, Holly and Thorns, 'scarlet of berries', all fully grown.

An advert was placed for the right to graze sheep in Clifton Park, tenders for crops in the field adjacent to Parkfield Road and the kitchen gardens to be let by tender.

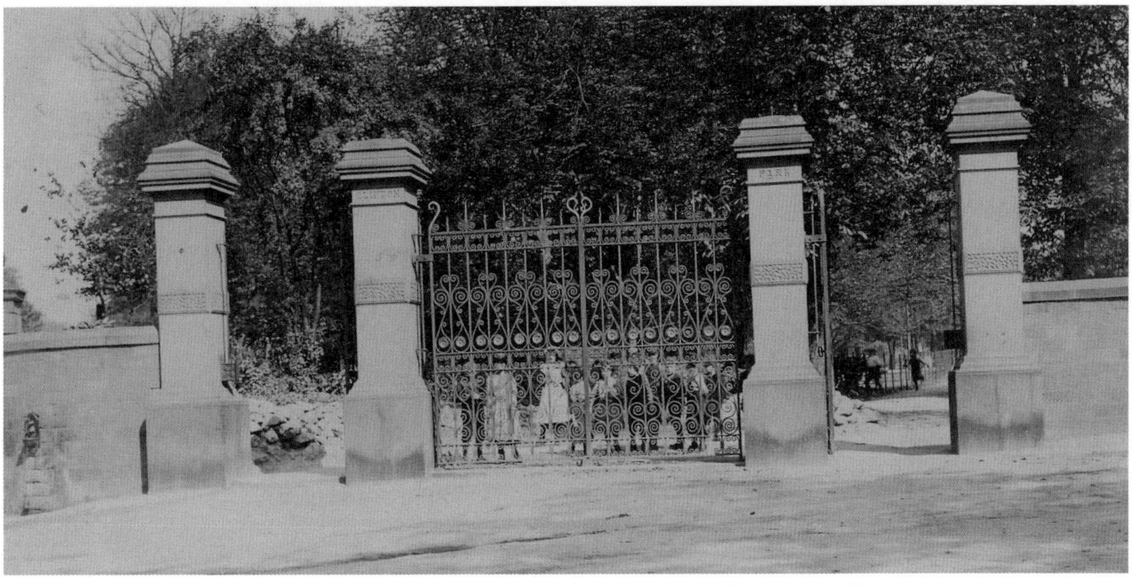
*Clifton Park gates at the junction of Doncaster Road and Clifton Lane. (Author's postcard)*

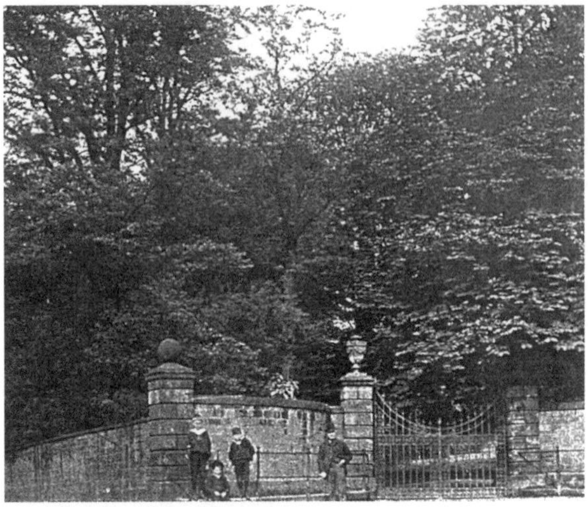

*Clifton Park gates 1891-1900*
*Original posts before moving them to the Clifton Grove entrance. (Rotherham Archives)*

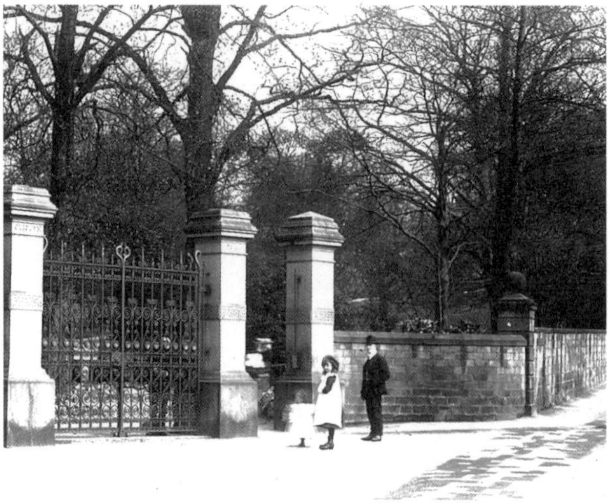

*Clifton Park gates 1911. (Author's postcard)*

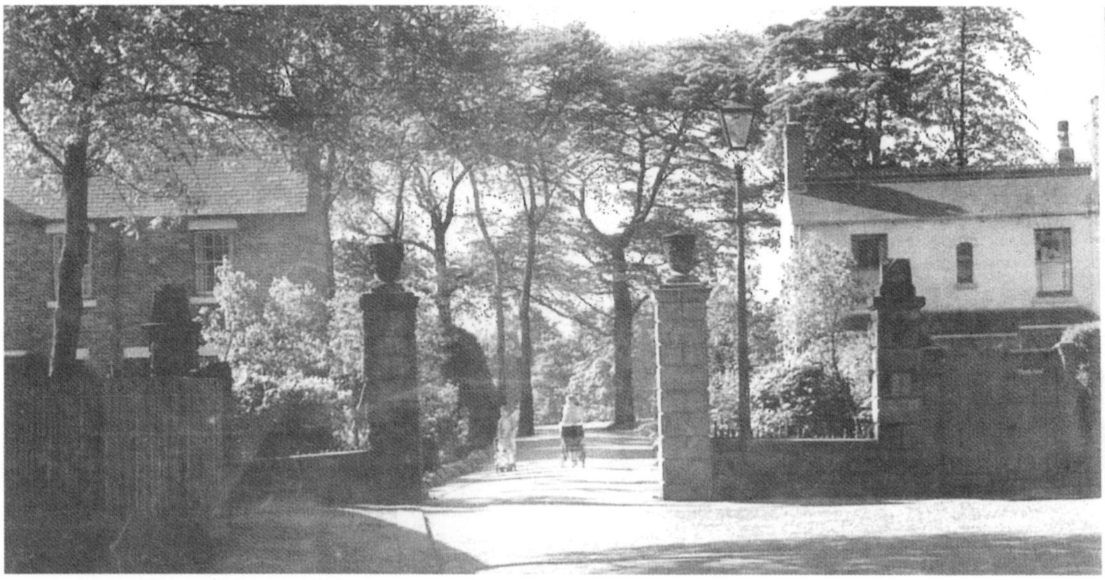

*Clifton Park entrance - Middleton Road / Clifton Grove 1960's. (Rotherham Archives)*

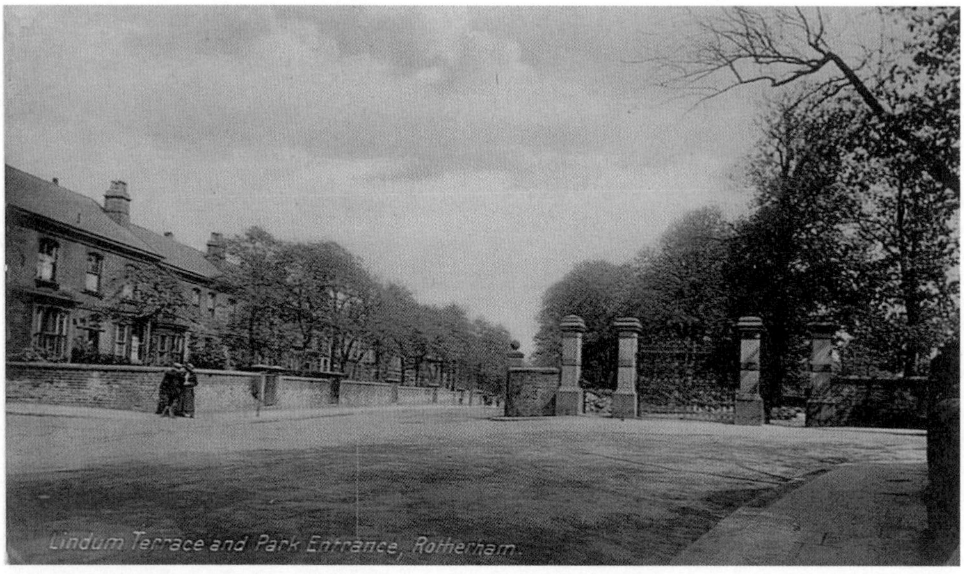


*The park gates following alteration of gates in the 1900's (Author's picture)*

In July 1891, Mr. Albaston, Junior, was appointed Curator, four men were transferred from Boston Park, and each issued with a Park Ranger cap. Later in the year, he was allowed to sell produce from the kitchen garden and keep accounts. By 1893, he had been promoted to Head Park Curator.

The park grew in popularity and in the summer of 1892, a Mr. Blagg was duly granted the right to supply refreshments. A request to give the old folks tea in the park was accepted, though the Band of Hope Union were not permitted to hold their gala but could use Boston Park instead! This was most likely due to all the alterations which were being carried out, and at that time, the park was no longer grazed.

In 1891, an additional entrance opposite Cottenham Road was made and the entrance at the Clifton Lane and Doncaster Road junction was redesigned. The original stone pillars were moved to the Clifton Grove / Middleton Road entrance that was also redesigned and Grade II listed in 1986. (Middleton Road previously called Jubilee Walk.)
Most of the work was completed by the summer season of 1893, but not all the contracts ran smoothly, indeed, some of the items were damaged and the construction of the bandstand was behind programme. A horse 15 hands high was purchased for all the heavy work.

As early as 1893, notices at the park entrances said "No Dogs allowed in the Park unless led by a string or chain" and football could only be played in prescribed areas.

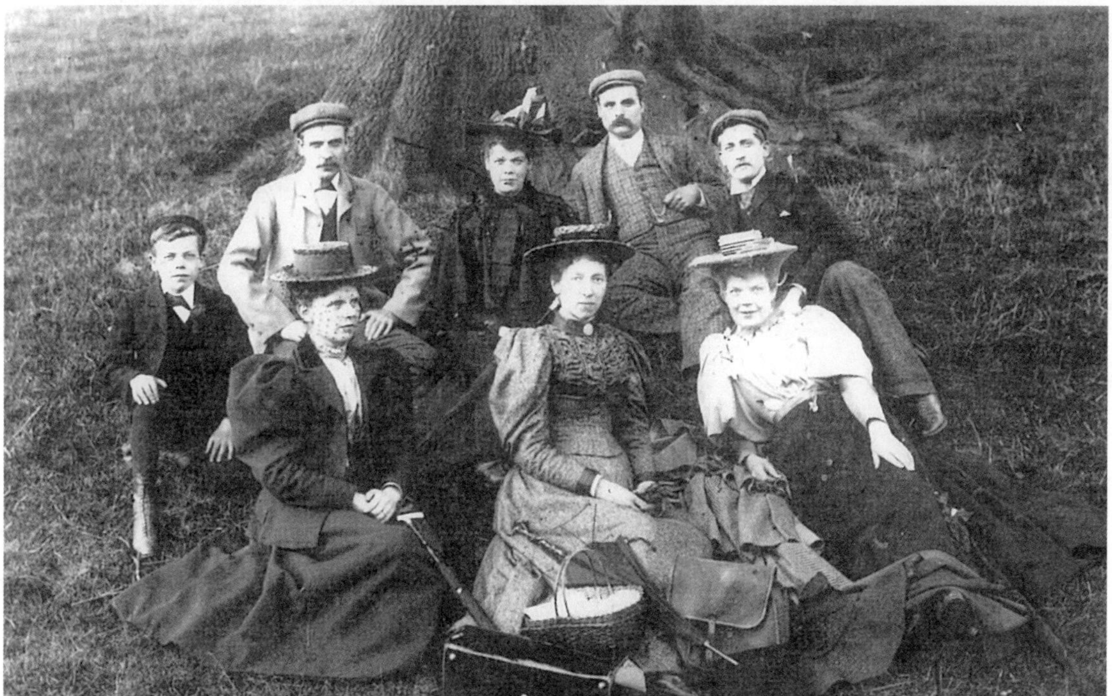

*Picnic time in Clifton Park. Circa 1900. (Rotherham Archives)*

By 1903, most of the recreation committee's ideas had been carried out and this included four miles of man-made walks.

In the Rotherham Advertiser on 7 July 1906, a lad of respectable appearance was summoned on a charge of entering Clifton Park by other than the authorised entrance on 29 June 1906. The Police Constable saw the boy climbing over some railings to get into the park on the occasion of the King's birthday celebrations.

In inflicting a fine of 5 shillings, including costs, the Chairman warned the defendant against breaking the park rules.

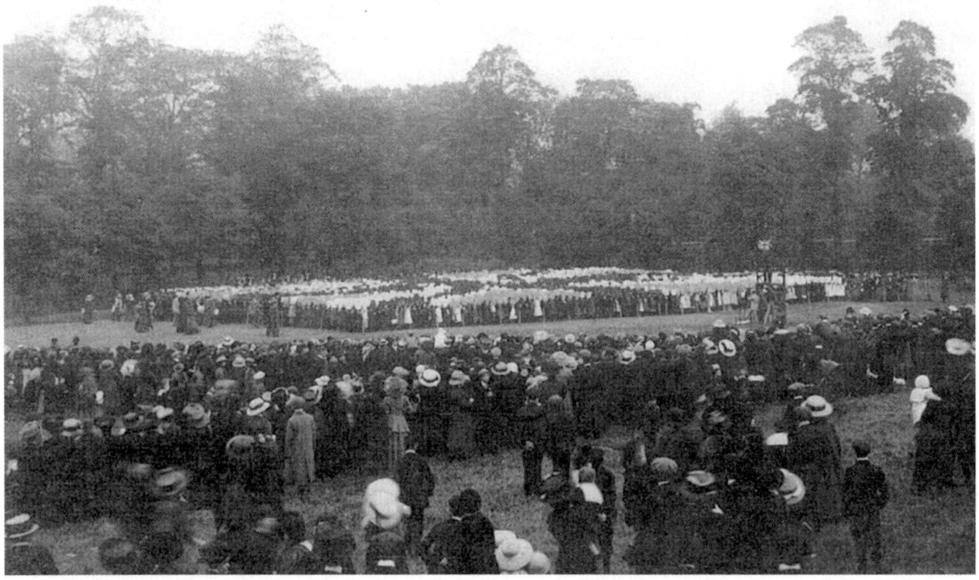

*Coronation celebrations in Clifton Park, 22nd June 1911. (Author's postcard)*

The main entrance was widened in 1915 and four stone pillars supported intricate wrought iron gates that were so large a brass wheel was attached for easy opening and closing. Yates & Haywood carried out the work on these gates for £14 and 5 shillings. Each evening the gates were secured and a bell was rung to warn visitors of this nightly ritual so they could leave the park.

In 1922, Mr Davis offered the council 10/- a day for the privilege of having a fruit stall in Clifton Park.

In 1931, the main pathways were lit by electricity. Many structural alterations have occurred in Clifton Park throughout the 124 years it has been Rotherham's premier park.

The old original gate posts at the back of the Museum at the Clifton Lane entrance were moved to the Middle Lane entrance many years ago.

The ornate gates at the main entrance and the railings around the park were removed for the War effort during the Second World War.

In 1964, a consultant's report threatened Clifton Park. It was suggested that St. Ann's Road would be developed and some of the new road would cut through the park. It escaped this severe chop but the Clifton Lane boundary wall was removed later in 1972 and the main entrance was taken further back to improve the road junction. Since that time, pedestrians and vehicle traffic can enjoy the view of Clifton Park.

Plan to provide a boating lake was shelved in 1973 as the allocation of money (£25,000) was thought to be insufficient.

In 1974, the old park entrance opposite Albany Street was closed and the larger entrance in front of the Museum was used instead as the volume of traffic on Clifton Lane was proving dangerous.

One of the ornamental lighting columns at the impressive main park entrance was smashed to pieces in a road traffic accident in 1974 and was impossible to replace. Terry Reeves, who began working for the town in 1964, skilfully repaired the columns and it is doubtful that anyone could detect the repair. Terry retired in March 2008.

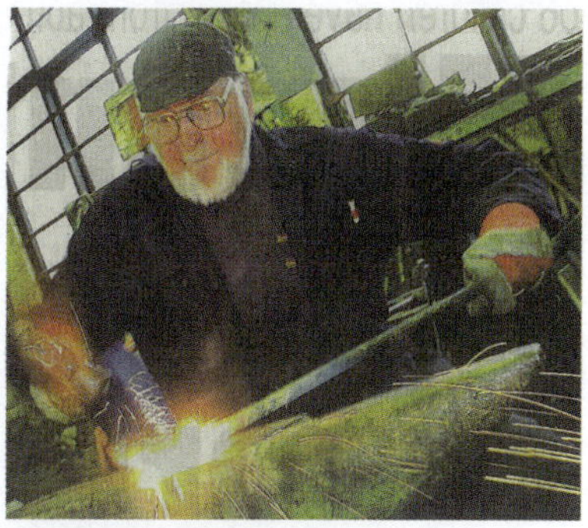

*Terry Reeves retiring after 43 years as a Blacksmith. (Rotherham Advertisier)*

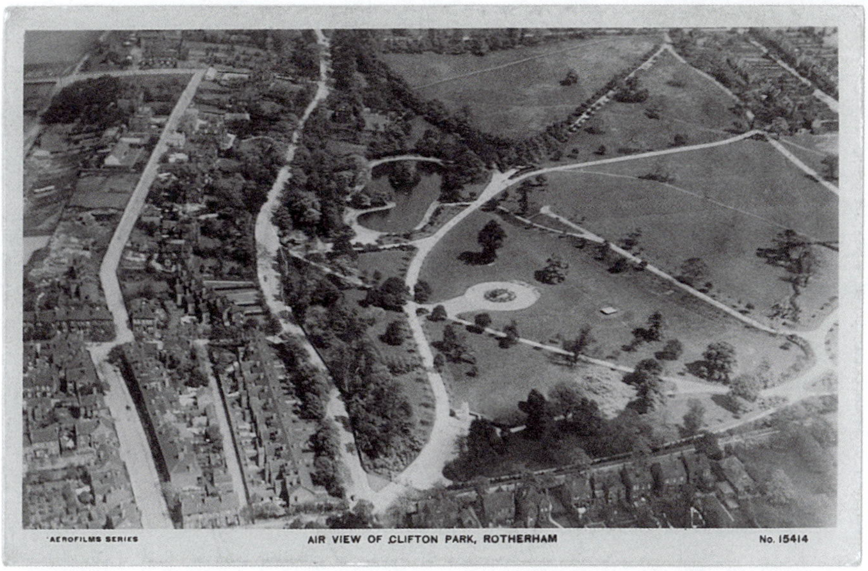


*Aerial photograph showing the lake, cenotaph and base of the bandstand. 1920's. (Author's postcard)*

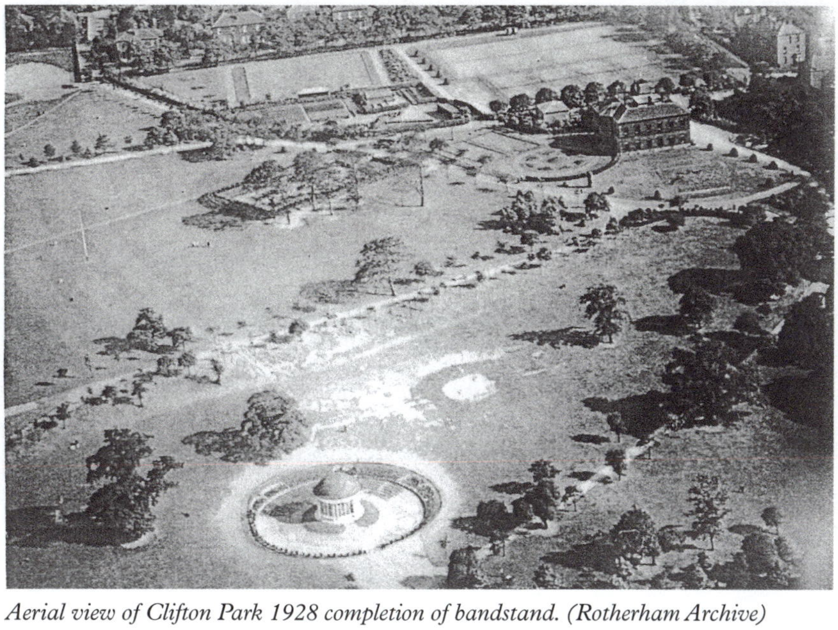

*Aerial view of Clifton Park 1928 completion of bandstand. (Rotherham Archive)*

# 3 CLIFTON PARK LAKE

A fishpond shown on the survey drawing of 1820 was constructed near to Doncaster Road. It provided fish for the table of Clifton House and ice for the icehouse, where both ice and food were stored. It also provided gentle recreation for the Walker family.

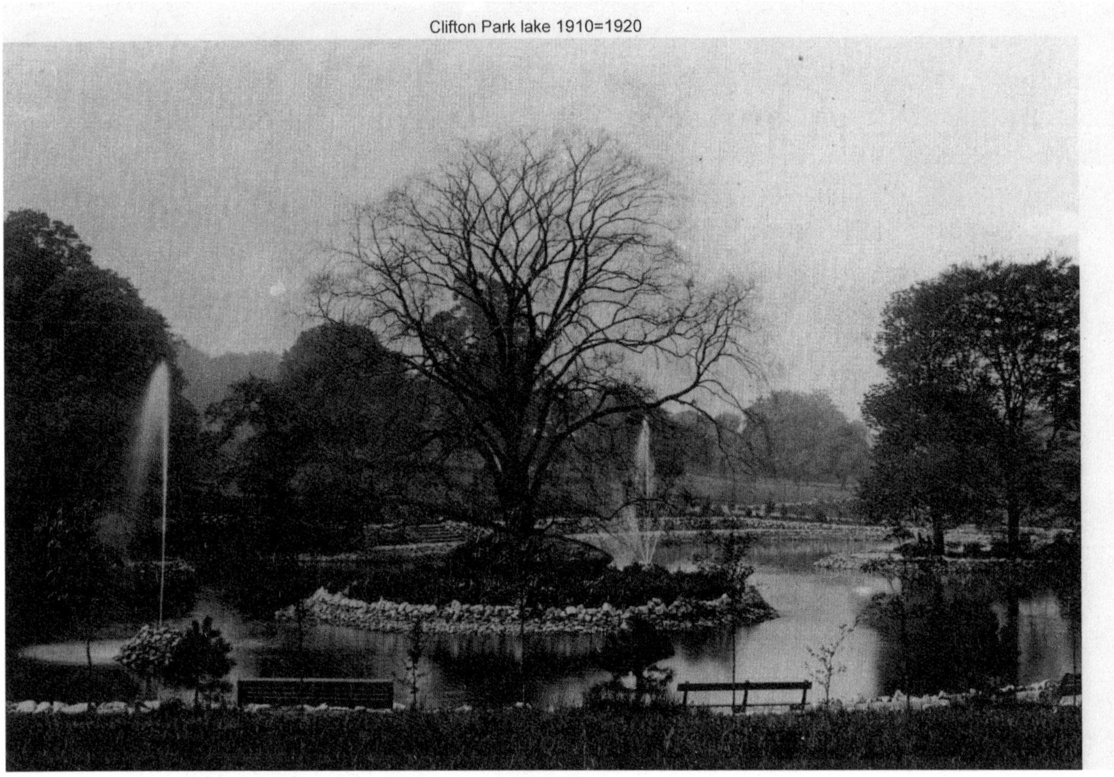


*The fountains in the lake, 1910 - 1920. (Rotherham Archives)*

Rotherham Corporation purchased the lake, which was an angler's paradise, from Mr E Drabble J. P. when they bought Clifton Estate. The fishpond was enlarged and become a lake in 1892. Although it was no more than 3 feet deep, it had an island in the middle for wildlife and three high fountains. A water main was laid to supply the fountains and the sewer near the lake was diverted around it. The lake was restocked with fish valuing £5 and fishing was very popular

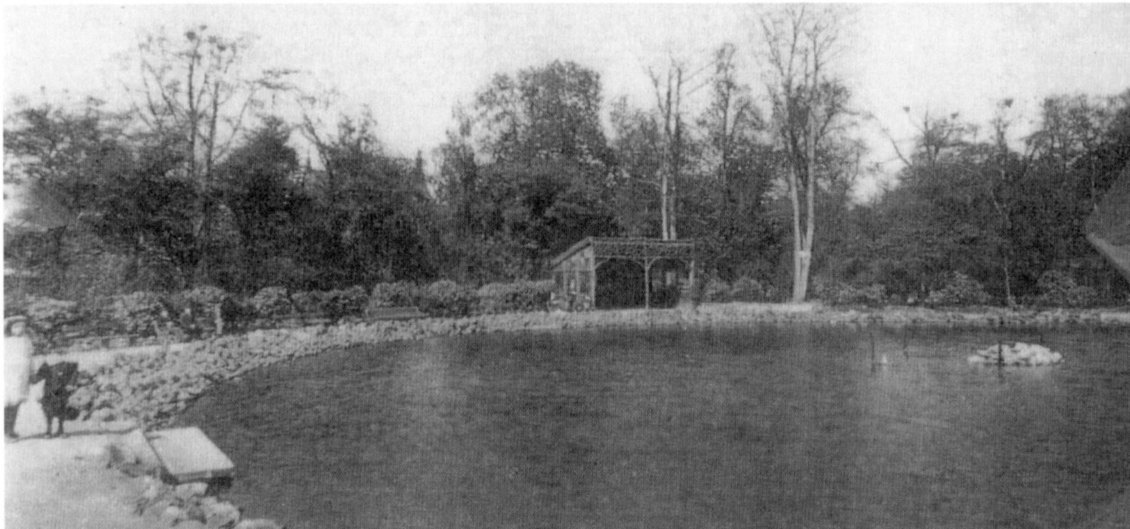

*Clifton Park lake showing the rustic shelter. (Rotherham Archives)*

When this mammoth task was completed, ice skating was then allowed on the lake in December 1892. Rustic shelters and drinking fountains were added for the skaters and spectators.

It must have been a very popular attraction because a policeman was in attendance to preserve and protect the trees and shrubs, including the wire netting which was provided for the protection of the wildfowl on the island. A lifeboat was also on standby.

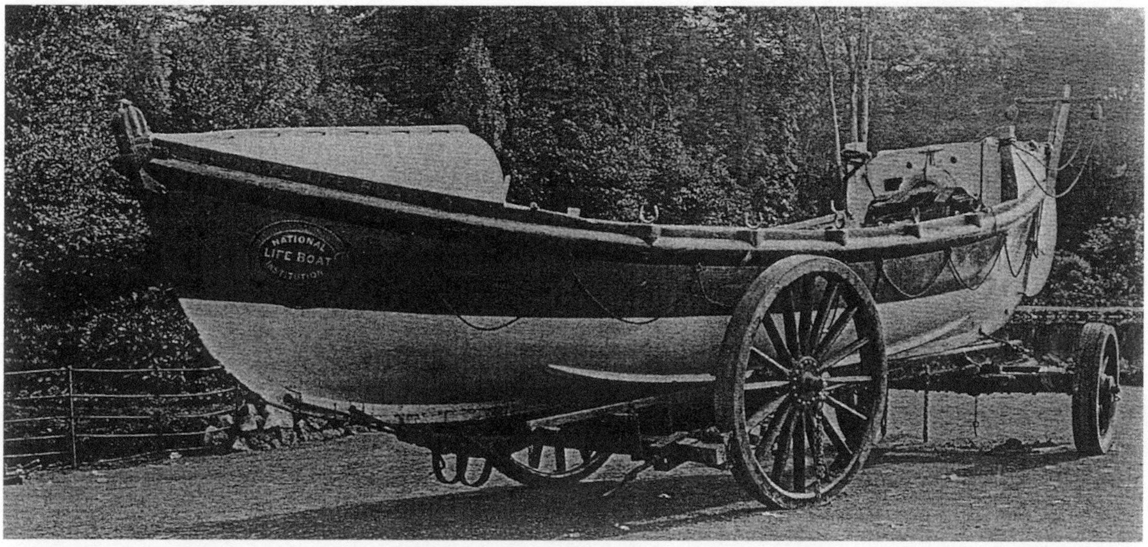

*Clifton Park lake lifeboat, Circa 1905. (Rotherham Archives)*

In the early 1900s, the winters were severe. In January 1902, there were heavy floods and to prevent the lake from overflowing, the valve at the bottom of the lake was opened; considerable amounts of fish were lost. One year later the heavy rain caused the lower end of the lake to give way and during its repair, the sides were raised by 18 inches. It had to be regularly cleaned out to remove the mud.

Spare ducks and geese from the lake were regularly culled and sold at auction. New birds were then donated by various people to the park in order to restock the lake.

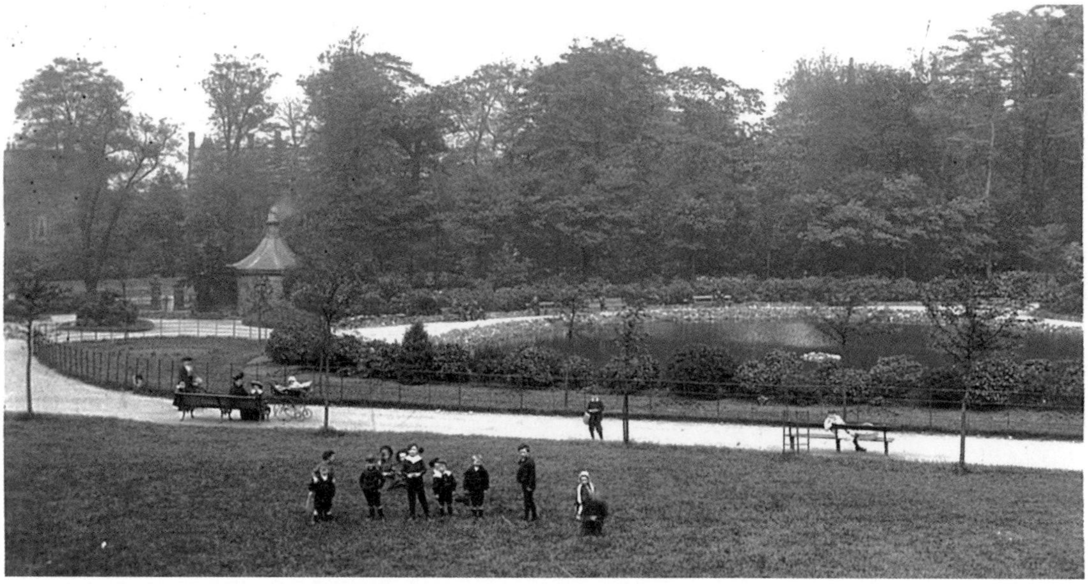

*The lake with Bird Cage Lodge in the background. (Author's postcard)*

In 1902, a letter from the Lord Chamberlain was received stating that the King had graciously complied with a request from the council for a swan to be placed on the lake, and asked the council to make arrangements for the removal of the swan from the River Thames to Rotherham. A swan's egg from the lake was placed in Clifton Park Museum. Later that year, the Earl Fitzwilliam gave a pair of Canadian geese. Other gifts to Clifton Park aviaries in the early 1900s included doves and peacocks.

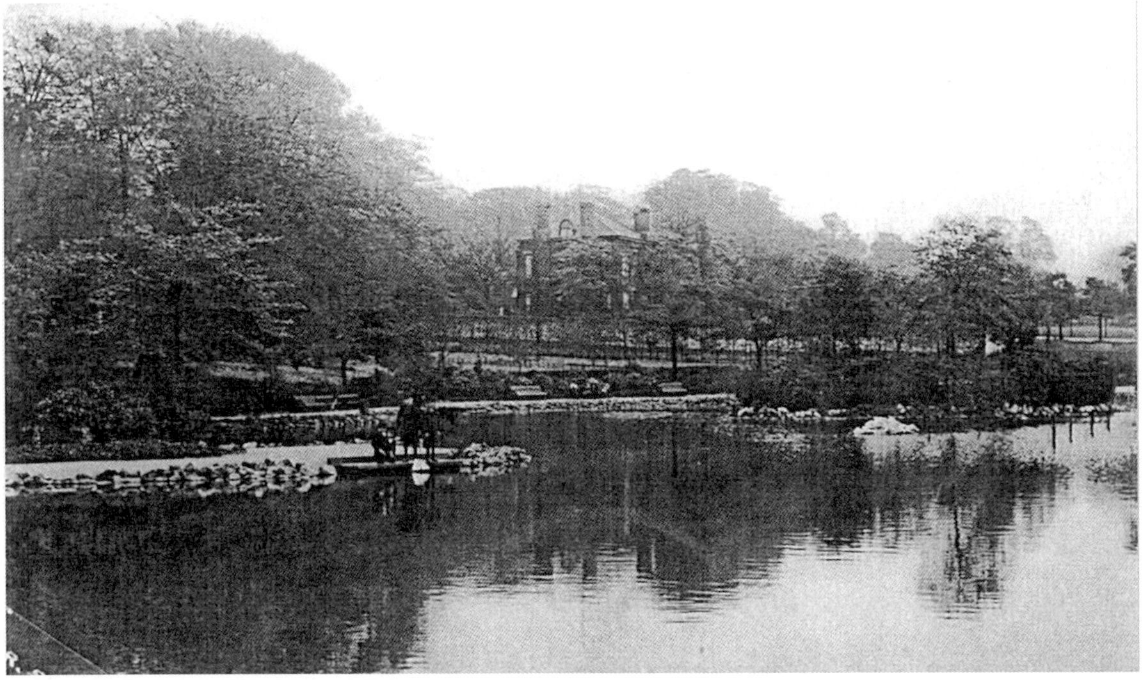

*The lake in Clifton Park. Park Lea is seen in the background. (Rotherham Archives)*

Water lilies from Wentworth Woodhouse and Rawmarsh Ponds at Parkgate were placed on the lake in 1903.

A shelter was built near the lake in 1910 to protect people from the rain; seating was very basic so visitors did not stay all day!

1913, a pair of Swans and three cygnets were transferred from the park and ducks were sold.

In February 1914, an interesting ceremony took place at the lake; Rotherham's first Motor Fire Engine proceeded through the streets to Clifton Park and attracted much interest. At the side of the lake, the pump action was tried and the Mayoress then smashed a bottle of water over it and named it 'Progress'.
In the 1930s, the town's new fire engines again entertained the crowds by taking water from the lake and shooting it into the air to test their capabilities!
It may come as a surprise to many that a large amount of the water came from the overflow of two sewers that drained surrounding higher districts. It was a victim of circumstances when housing estates were developed.

In 1935, it was suggested that the lake could be converted into a bathing pool.

Ice skating remained a popular winter pastime up until 1937 when it was decided that the lake should be drained, as it was 'unsanitary'. It is said that during its demolition, the houses around the park lake were overrun with rats!

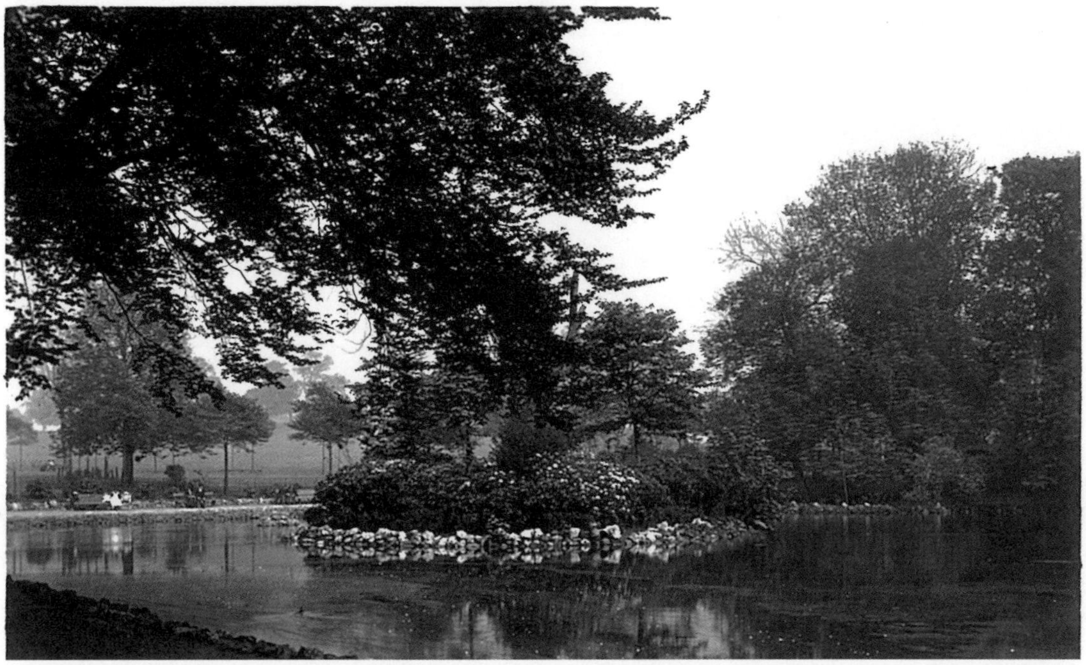

*The Island in the lake. (Author's postcard)*

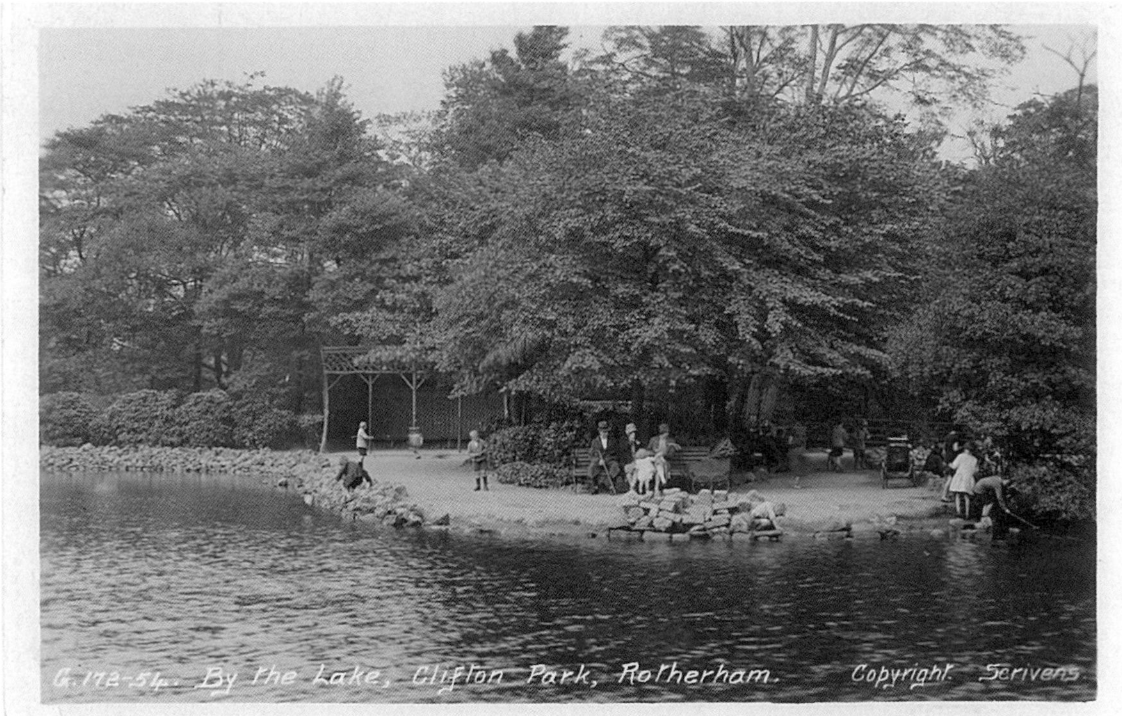


*Families strolling around the lake, 1932. (Author's postcard)*

## ROTHERHAM ADVERTISER 22 APRIL 1914

*Rough chipping placed on the path around the lake have caused discomfort to the thousands of people who use the park. Surely a finer material could be used and rolled in. This part of the park is very popular and visited by large numbers of residents whose boot soles are none too thick and in some cases, boots are missing altogether. Under these conditions, one at least expects a little consideration to be given to these people.*

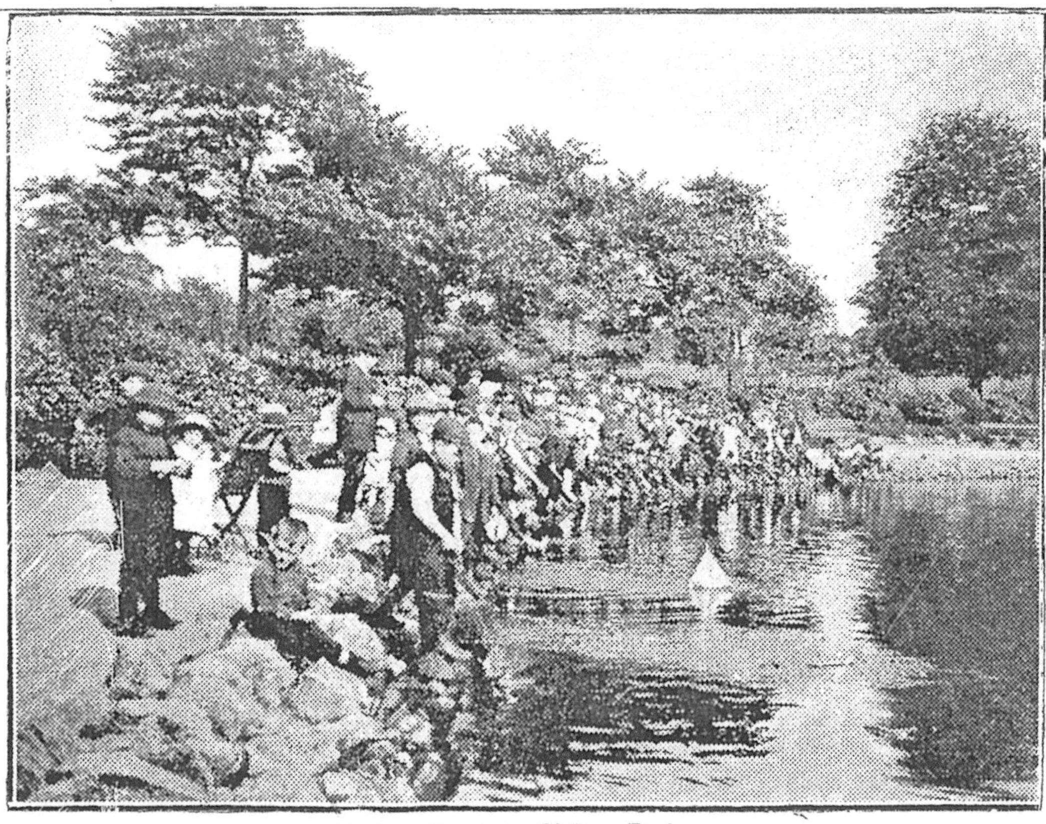

Sailing Boats in Clifton Park.

*Children sailing boats on Clifton Park lake. (Rotherham Archives)*

## 4 THE ICE HOUSE

The Ice House served Clifton House and was built near the second walled garden near the Clifton Grove entrance. It was used in conjunction with the fishpond.

It would have been carefully managed through the winter months; the fishpond would have been the best source of ice for the family, the still water would freeze much faster that the nearby river and there would be less pollution.

The ice once collected was packed into a partially sunk oval building with a domed roof and shaded by trees. It usually had an entrance passage with an inner and an outer door. Different instalments of ice would be laid with straw between them and the passage was then filled with insulating material. Ice houses were used occasionally to store game and fruit in pots.

Clifton Estate Ice House is shown on the 1894 plans but nothing remains of it today. It is thought that the sewer, which was laid through the park downwards towards the fishpond, could have interfered with the operation of the pump or affected the Ice House drainage.

## 5 THE WALLED GARDEN

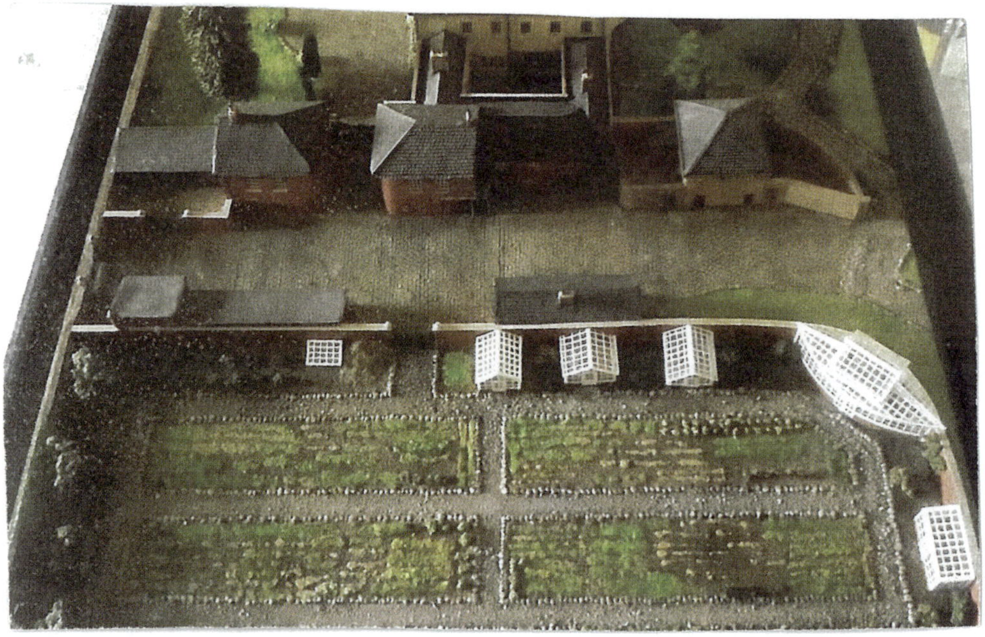

*This model of the walled garden can be seen inside the Museum. (Author's postcard)*

The Walled Garden to the side of Clifton house had a range of glasshouses and a curved building that could have been an orangery for rearing tender plants. A large stone trough, still to be seen in the park, would have been used for water collection. A drying area for clothes was nearby.

The many quarries around Rotherham could have provided stone for the garden walls, but earlier gardeners had discovered that brick retained heat and it was better for the production of fruit. It allowed protection of the fruit blossom from frost and better ripening of it. It should be remembered that stone was still an expensive commodity and damaged easily.

The fruit trees were held to the wall with hand-made nails tied to the branches with 'shreds' (little strips of cloth which were renewed each season). As a result of this, the wall joints were soon pitted with nail holes and the lime mortar pointing had to be renewed on a regular basis.

A second Walled Garden was situated near the Clifton Grove entrance; planted with plants which were not as 'sweet-smelling' and could have required hot beds.

The Walled Garden was removed in 1892.

The first record of an Estate Gardener appears in the 1841 census.
An old brick potting shed built in the early 1900s, on the site of the Walled Garden, was demolished in 2008. D&S Clark manufactured the bricks used; they were the brick makers of Milton Street and Arthur Street, Masborough, Rotherham, between 1887 and 1906.

The wall at Badsley Moor Lane Hospital was also demolished at around the same time and it was built with bricks from the same company.

# 6 BIRD CAGE LODGE

In the 1830s, significant changes were made within the Georgian park that included the building of a lodge and driveway on Doncaster Road. It served as a main entrance and provided a gracious carriage approach to the house.

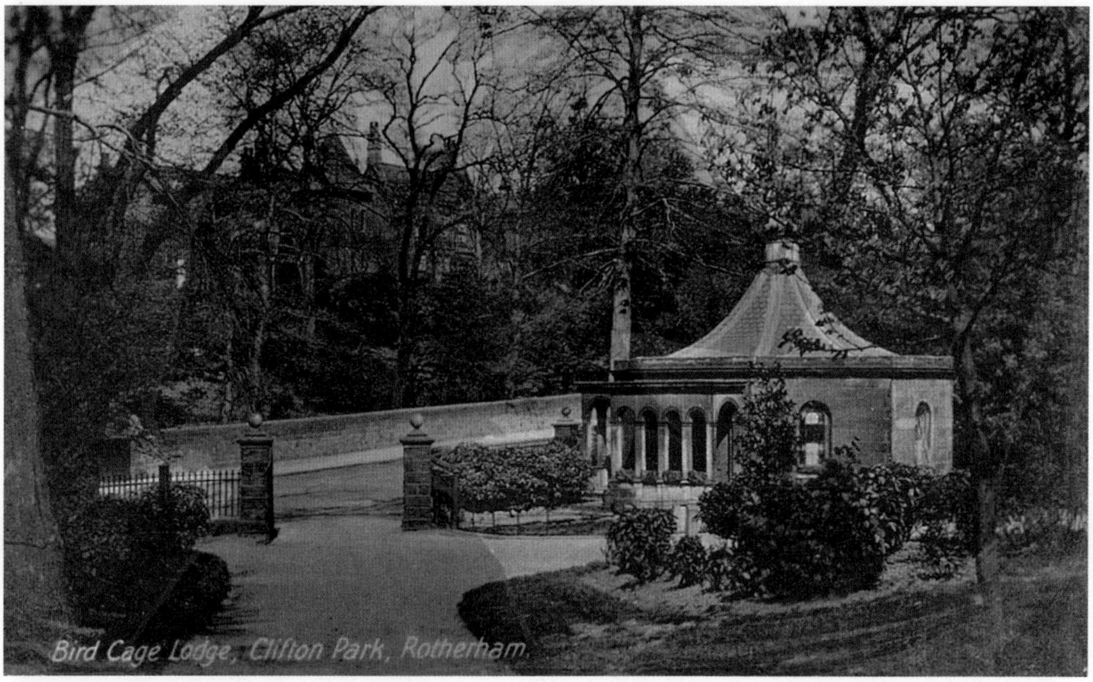


*Bird Cage Lodge, 1914. (Author's postcard)*

Bird Cage Lodge, primarily known as Clifton Lodge, served as the Lodge House for the Clifton Estate of the Walker Family; also referred to as Walker's Lodge.

In the middle of the 19th Century across the road from the Lodge, was a cottage belonging to Doctor Knight, which was in the style of a birdcage, it is thought that this is how the name came about. Rotherham Corporation altered this entrance after the purchase.

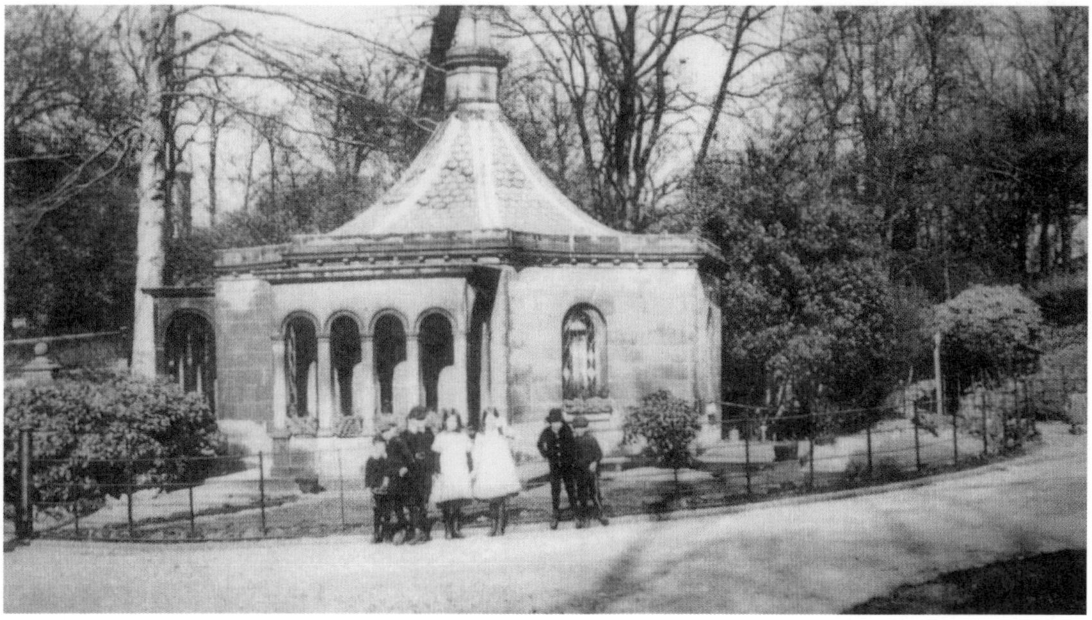

*Bird Cage Lodge, 1915. (Rotherham Archives)*

From 1891, the Lodge was used as accommodation for various park keepers and gardeners and there is a great deal of local knowledge of families living in Bird Cage Lodge.

Henry Hanby, born in 1850, was a Park Keeper and Grounds man and resided in the lodge in 1891. His name appears on the rate books for that time.

18th January 1892 Mr Roots, the first Park Ranger, lived there rent free in addition to his wages of 22/- per week.
Fred Cooke and his wife lived there in 1901.

Arthur Newsum was born there in December 1919 at Bird Cage Lodge whilst his Father was employed as one of the resident Park Keepers.

Barbara Shippam (nee Wilkes) was born there in 1935 when her father was a Gardener.

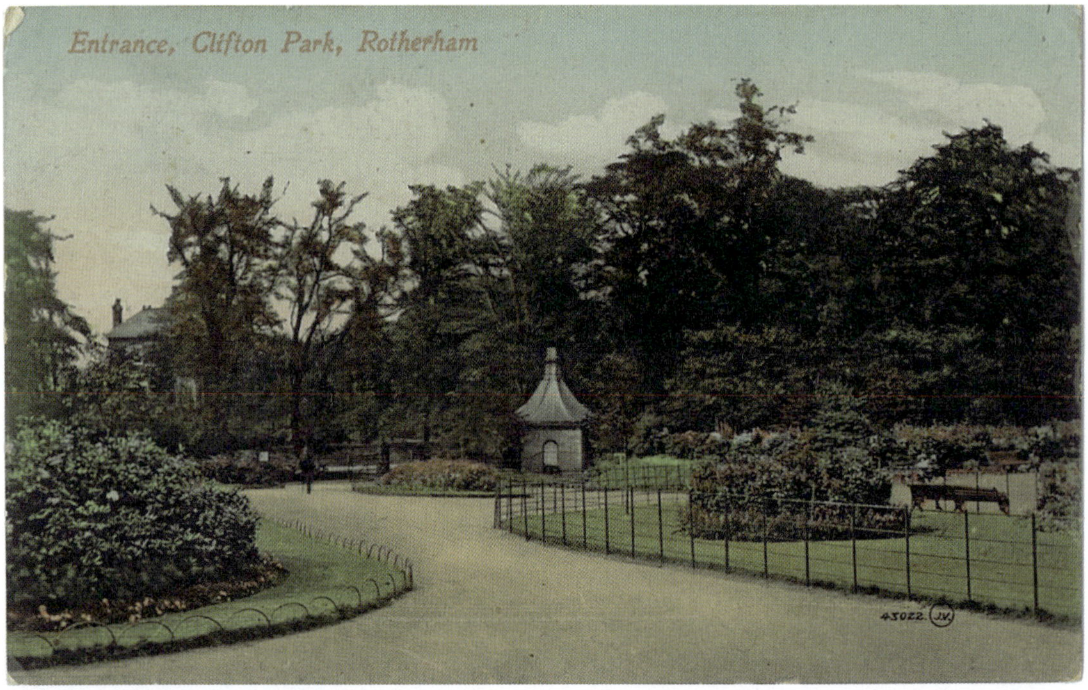


*Bird Cage Lodge, entrance 1926. (Author's postcard)*

These are only a few of the people who lived there but in October 1946, the Lodge was considered unfit for any purpose and within a few months, it was demolished. The garden of the Lodge was developed into a small, quiet area known as the Dell.

## 7 ORIENTAL CAFÉ

On Whit Monday 1921, Henry Gough Ltd opened the Oriental Café to the public. It was in the building adjoining the Museum with the windows on one side looking out over the tennis lawn and the other towards Clifton Lane. There was a further room to be used as an extension to the café.

A permanent kiosk was established outside, near the bowling greens, so people did not have to walk inside for their sweets, buns and refreshments. On summery days, tea would be served around tables near the tennis lawn by waitresses dressed in very attractive pale blue dresses.

There was seating for 100 people altogether in the café where teas and other refreshments are served daily from 2 pm until 8 pm. Clifton Park an ideal place for rest and recreation.

## 8 THE GROTTO

On the 1853 Ordnance Survey, an area marked 'rockery' was the site of the Grotto or artificial cave. Adorned with ferns and geological specimens worthy of preservation including coral and shells

There is very little knowledge of it, but is recorded in early photographs placing it at the southeast corner, near the Kitchen Garden to the side of the Museum.

The Grotto had disappeared by 1923.

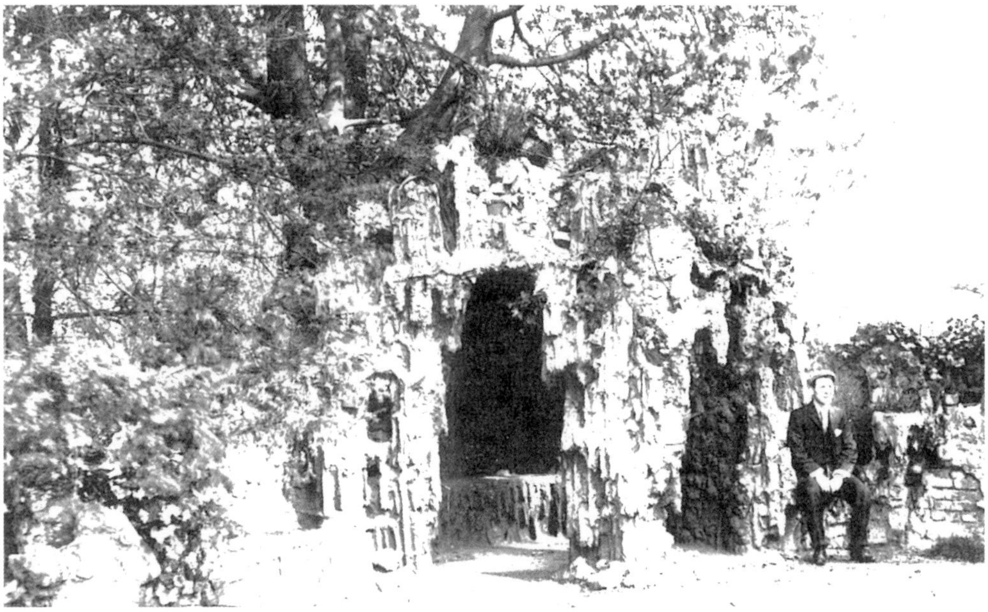

*The Grotto showing the intricate design. (Rotherham Archives)*

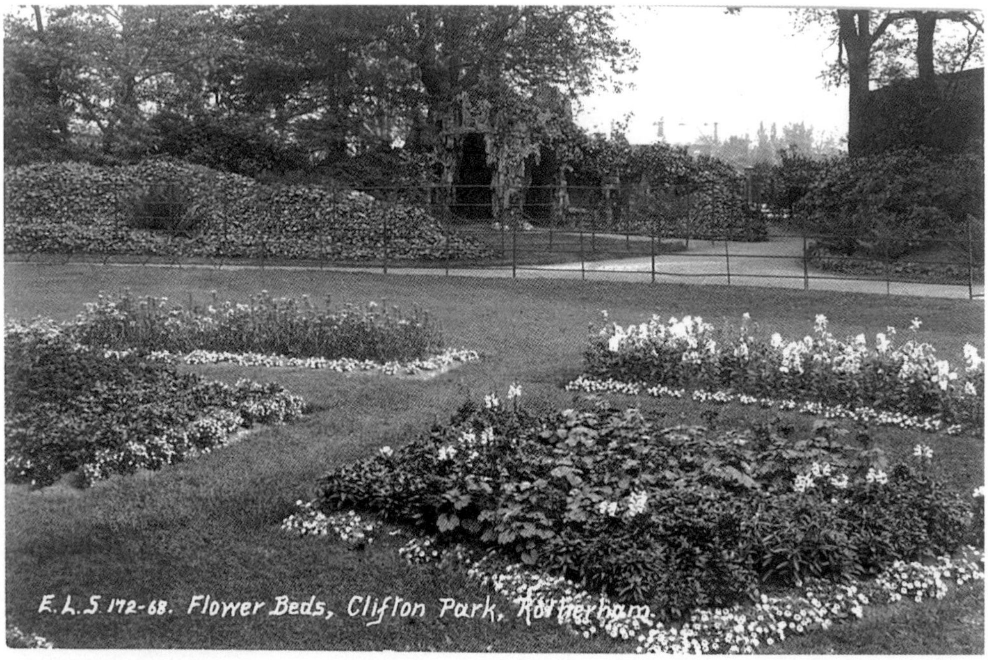


*The Grotto. The corner of the Museum can be seen to the right and Clifton Lane is in the background. (Author's postcard)*

## 9 THE SCARP WALK

The Scarp Walk ran from the Pleasure Grounds around the House, along the ridge and down to the fishpond.

This path allowed the family and their visitors to promenade through the estate and look over the lower drive on to Doncaster Road to the right and the Parish Church, known as the Minster since 2004, to the left.

The Walker family's finest animals could be viewed from their carriages on the paths and as they took the air along the Scarp Walk.

In July 1891, fifty seats were set out along the Scarp Walk under the trees so that visitors could enjoy the music in the Bandstand. In the 1940s and 1950s, many local people called the Scarp Walk the 'Monkey Run'.

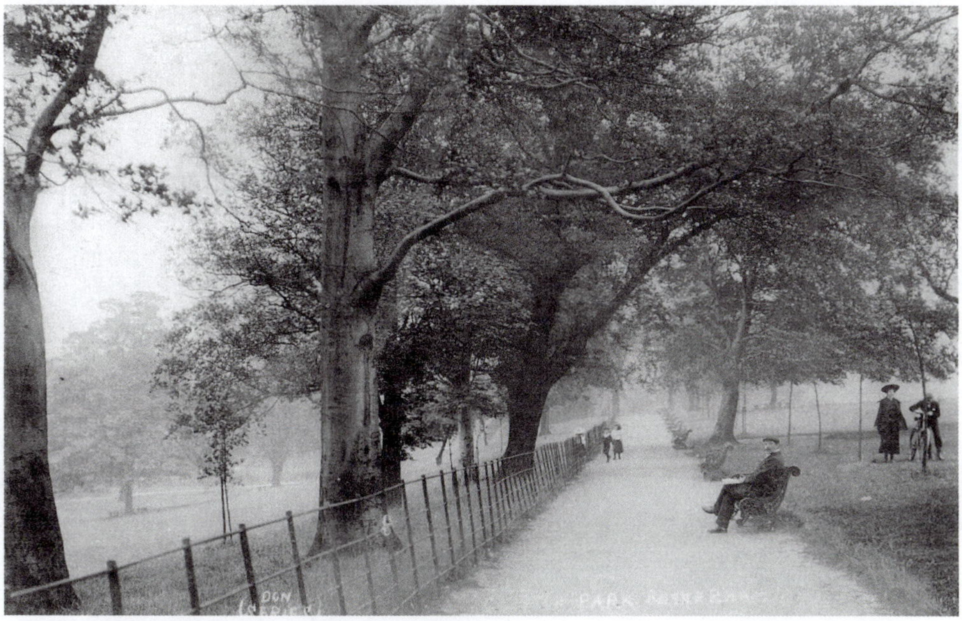

*The Scarp Walk, 1902 - 1904. (Rotherham Archives)*

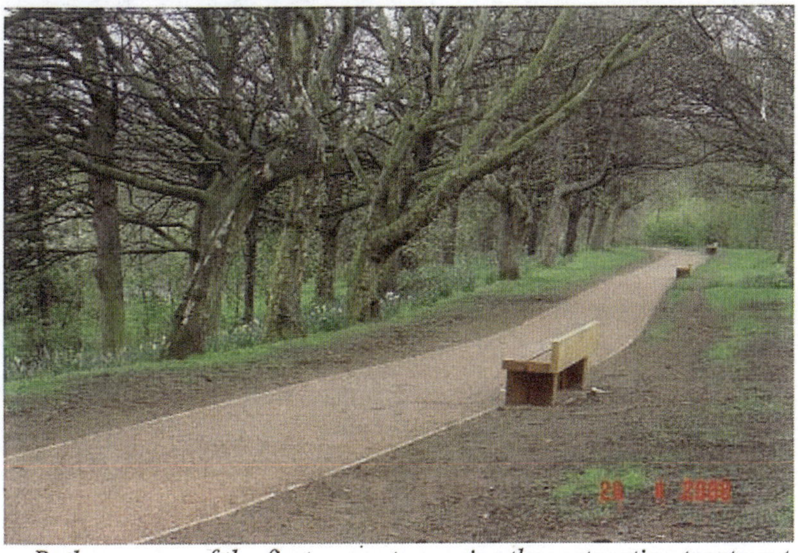

*The Scarp Path was one of the first areas to receive the restoration treatment and was completed earlier in 2008.*

## 10 THE WORLD WAR I APPEAL

In April 1915, in response to an appeal to raise additional brigades of artillery, the Mayor and council recruiting committee undertook to raise a Howitzer Brigade of 4 batteries and 633 men.

By 15 May 1915, the 164th (Rotherham) Howitzer Brigade, Royal Field Artillery, was up to complement and a large number of horses given for the Brigade's use.

Initial training was held in Clifton Park, to the detriment of tree and plants. A large area was taken over and used as a riding school.

There were many sightseers and two police officers put on duty. The Commanding Officer's headquarters and battery store used two rooms at the rear of Clifton House.

The 12 June 1915 was a military day and the Mayor, Mr. T. W. Grundy, reviewed a grand military parade with 4,000 troops and a military band. This was followed by a recruiting meeting in the tram sheds on Rawmarsh Road and was addressed by the Bellicose Horatio Bottomley, Editor of the John Bull.

At the same time, the YMCA established a recreation tent for the use of soldiers billeted in Rotherham. It was for writing and reading and had a concert room with a platform at one end. A piano was provided and the refreshment bar was not forgotten.

The Howitzer Brigade left Rotherham in July 1915 for further training elsewhere in Yorkshire and on Salisbury Plain.

By January 1916, all these men were at the front in France.

The Rotherham Advertiser, July 1915, published a poem from a soldier on the front line:-

*THE HOWITZER BRIGADE*
*SENT FROM THE FRONT IN BELGIUM BY PRIVATE MITCHELL*

*When the call for men was sounding*
*And the country's prospect grave,*
*Who could have come up better*
*Than the Howitzer Brigade.*

*They came from town and village*
*With hearts so brave and true,*
*To show the other fellows*
*What the Howitzers could do.*

*And in a park at Rotherham*
*They train with all their might*
*Oh! If Kaiser Bill could see them*
*Wouldn't he get a fright.*

*And day by day they're training*
*For their country and their King,*
*And when they have to leave us*
*We'll make the whole town ring.*

*And the friends whom they are leaving*
*Will think of them and say –*
*"God bless the boys who fight for us*
*And bring them back some day."*

*And when the war is over*
*And a brilliant victory won,*
*We'll be the first to greet them*
*And say what they have done.*

*So three cheers for the boys of Rotherham*
*Who have joined the R. F. A.*
*And our blessings will be with them*
*All the time that they're away.*

# 11 THE WAR MEMORIAL

The war memorial in Clifton Park is very imposing and overlooks a busy crossroads and beautiful gates at its main entrance. It is also very close to the town centre.

A local architect, Lt. Col. James Edward Knight, born in Rotherham in 1867 and had himself seen active service, designed it. The London cenotaph in Whitehall had inspired him.

The cenotaph and the curtain wall behind it are constructed of Bolton Woods sandstone that varies in colour from fawn to light grey and is quarried near Bradford in West Yorkshire.

The design included the use of a lead pipe downwards through the centre connected with other drainage on the ledges. The rainwater flows through the troughs preventing weathering and discolouration of the warm buff surfaces. You can compare this against the green stained wreaths and swords on the cenotaph to see its success.

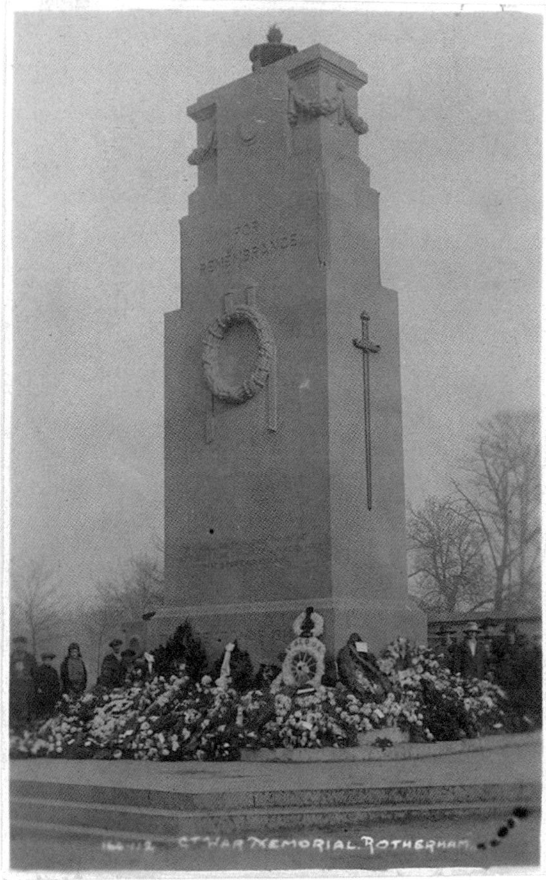

*1922 dedication of the Great War Cenotaph. (Author's postcard)*

The surrounds and steps of the war memorial are dark greenmoor stone from coal measures strata, quarried at Shepley near Huddersfield.

The cost of building this impressive structure was borne by the War Memorial Committee. Three designs were considered and the chosen one was 26 feet high and cost £50,000. On top of the Cenotaph was a lamp brazier of bronze, the flame of which shown to be constantly lit to typify the undying and unquenchable glory of the gallant dead.

Work began in 1919 to draw up the list of 1,304 names that were to be put onto the twelve bronze plates on the curtain wall. Each of these Rotherham men belonged to 88 units of the armed forces.

Two names of men who returned from WW1 are actually engraved on the Cenotaph, one being Fred Fell. He enlisted in the 5th Battalion York and Lancs, 1914 aged 17½ years. Three years later, he was reported wounded and missing. His mother received a letter from the War Office stating he was killed in action. Eighteen months later he returned. In fact, he had been taken prisoner of war for the duration. The War Office for their terrible mistake issued a letter of apology.

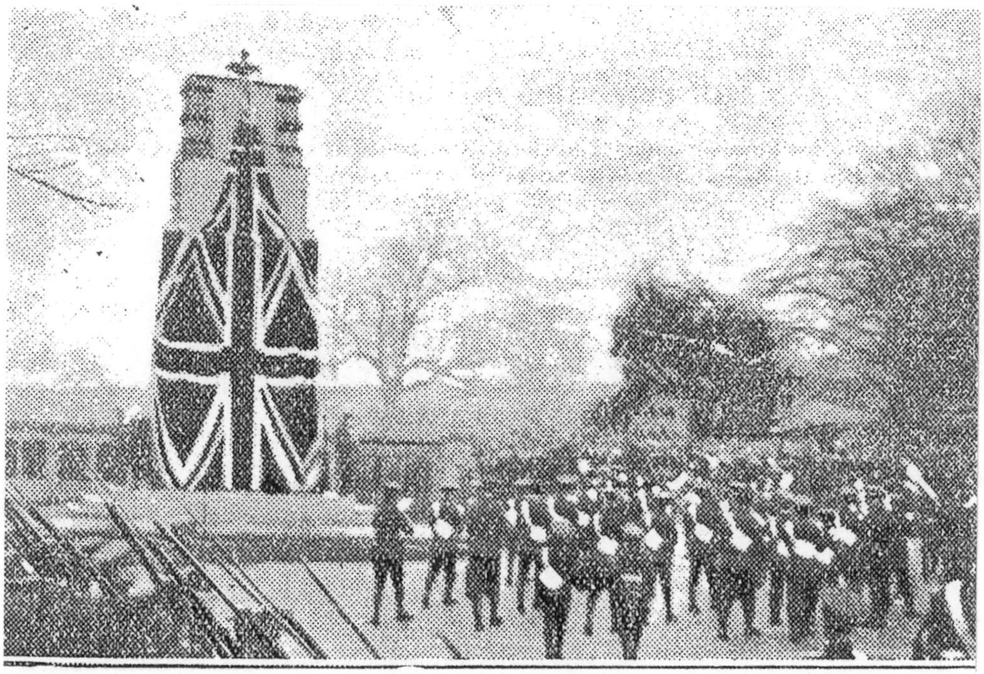

*Dedication of the World War I war memorial. (Rotherham Archives)*

It was unveiled on 26 November 1922 by the First World War general, General Sir (Frederick) Ivor Maxse, KCB, CVO, DSO, (22 December 1862 – 1958), in the presence of the Bishop of Sheffield who gave the dedication. At the unveiling ceremony, Alderman G Gummer announced that over £13,750 had been promised to the fund and that after meeting liabilities £8,000 would remain. When collected this would form the nucleus of a fund for further memorial in the provision of a new Casualty and Out Patient's Department at the Rotherham Hospital.

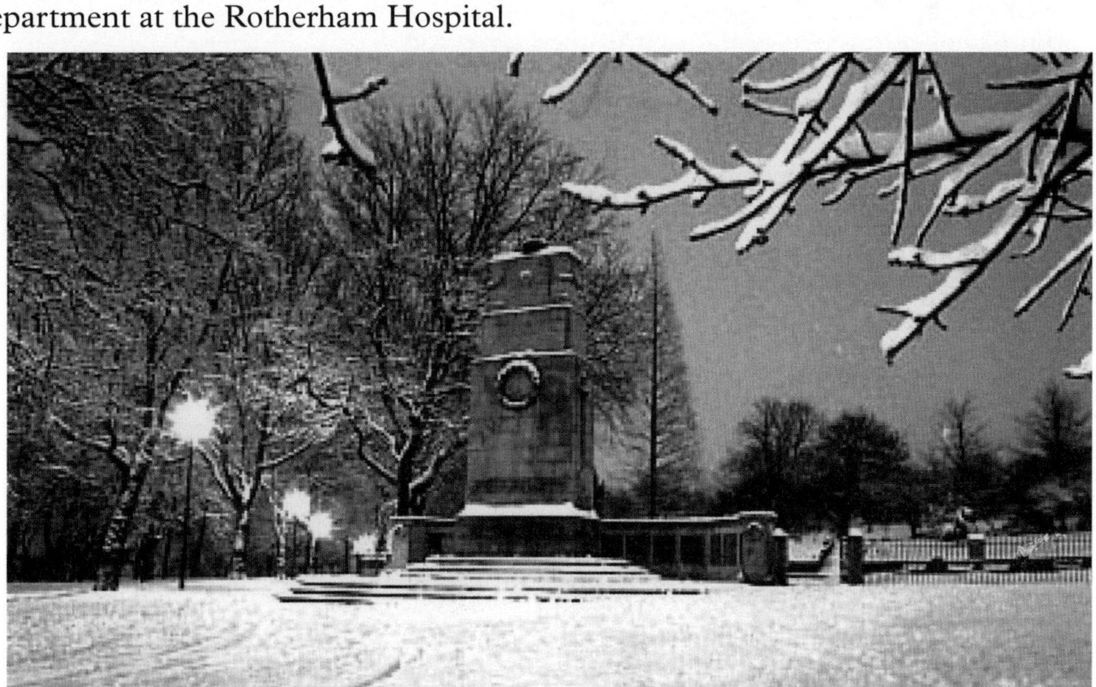

*The Cenotaph on a snowy day before restoration. (Rotherham Family History Society)*

Each November since this date, the people of Rotherham pay homage to the fallen of World War 1 and later World War 2.

# 12 THE GARDEN OF REMEMBRANCE

Remembrance gardens + cenotaph, Clifton Park 1954=1955

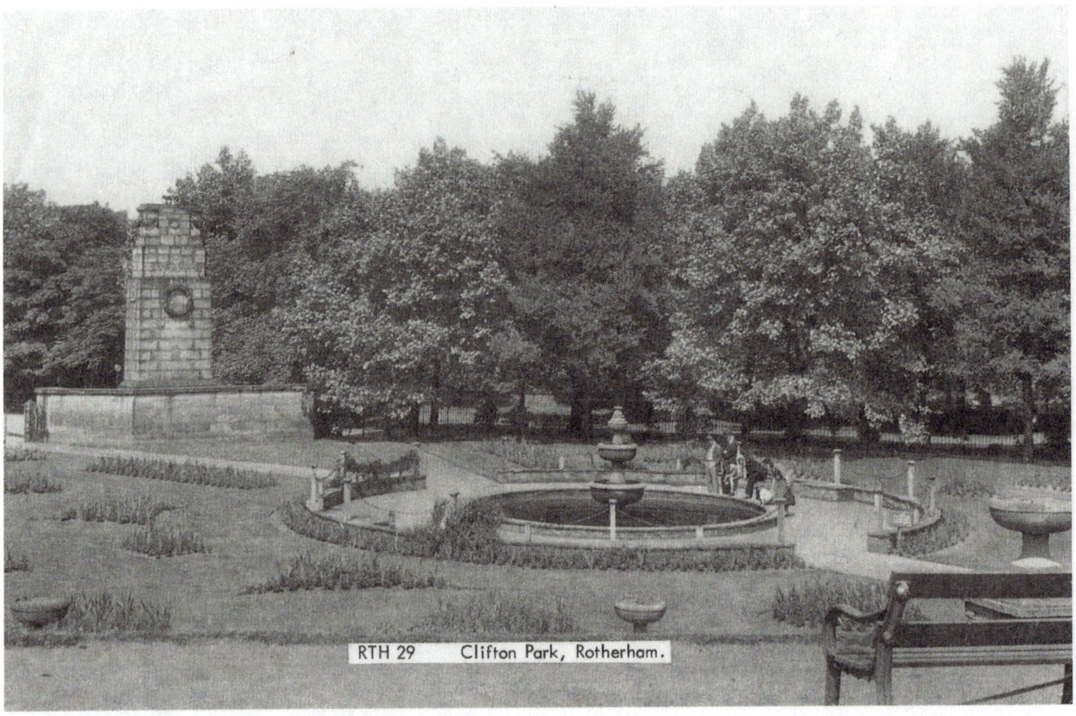


*The memorial garden, 1954 - 1955. (Rotherham Archives)*

The 'Garden of Meditation', fondly called the Memorial Garden by the people of Rotherham, was developed to the rear of the Cenotaph.

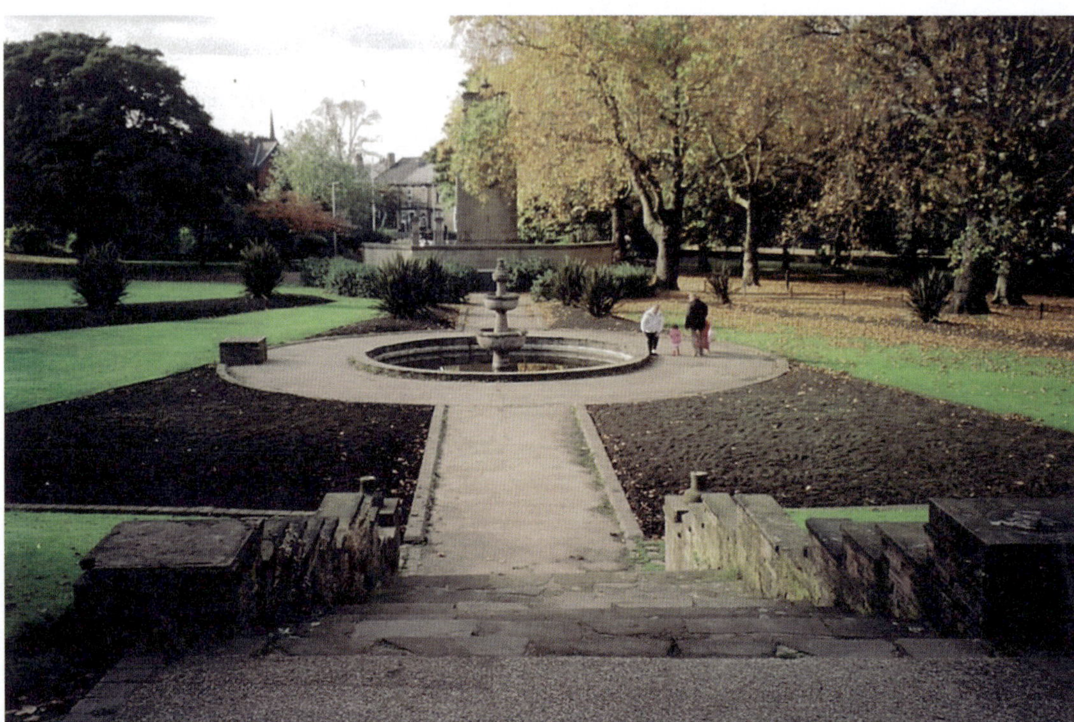

*Memorial garden in autumn 2007. (Author)*

It is laid out as a formal garden; the flowerbeds radiating from a central stone fountain. Water flowed over the central bowls into a circular pool containing goldfish. Seating around the garden, between the plinths and on top of the terracing provided a peaceful place to rest.

On each plinth, below the urns, are the names of each service to which the garden was dedicated: -

| | |
|---|---|
| United Nations | W.R.N.S |
| Royal Navy | Civil Defence |
| E.N.S.A. | Workers |
| Army | Housewives |
| Colonies | A.T.S. |
| Royal Air Force | Nursing Services |
| Merchant Navy | W.A.A.F. |
| W.V.S. | Home Guard |
| Police | NAAFI |
| India | St. Johns' Ambulance |
| Royal Observer Corps. | War Savings Ass. |

Beautiful flowers in abundance changed with the season in the flowerbeds and in the urns on top of the plinths.

The stone was carved locally by Brian Jones. He was a Master Craftsman and Stonemason and helped to make the impressive fountain when he was an apprentice at a local quarry.

In a moving ceremony, the Minister of Defence, Mr A.V. Alexander on Sunday 25th July 1948, opened the garden. The Vicar of Rotherham, Bishop G.V. Gerard, conducted the service of dedication. The sun blazed down on groups of service units and pre-service representatives, whilst the guard of honour was inspected.

The Mayor, Mr C. Bosworth, made an appeal to the people of Rotherham to honour and respect the garden as it belonged to them. Mr Alexander concluded his speech saying "I pray this garden may be a garden of Meditation, let us labour in the memory of those whom we loved and lost to make this world a better place".

The K.O.Y.L.I. Band played and trumpeters from the R.A.F. played the 'Last Post' and 'Reveille'.

August 1949 more than 500 lights were used to illuminate the Memorial Garden. It was the closing week for 'Holidays at Home', it attracted large crowds and luckily, the weather was good. At the end of the week, there was a grand firework display

In September 1952, the Memorial Garden was illuminated once again. During Christmas 1953, a Christmas tree was lit up.

# 13 THE MEMORIAL ROCK GARDEN

This beautiful garden lies behind the Memorial Garden and was opened by the Mayor, Councillor A.R. Shaylor on 19 August 1951. It was the creation of the parks superintendent, Mr. William Goodall and cost £2,000. He retired from work in 1955, 3 years after the garden was opened

800 tons of stone, quarried at Hooton Levitt, with some of the stones weighing as much as 8 tons, formed a rock face with a waterfall cascading into a small pool containing goldfish; a bridge with shallow steps crossed this pool. A rill on either side of a central lawn ran downwards, it collected at the bottom and pumped upwards again to feed the waterfall. The pathways were laid with 100 tons of stone crazy paving and eight rustic seats placed around. In September 1952, the garden was illuminated for a short while.

There is one memorial stone in the Rock Garden, placed there with a seat in 1964, dedicated to Mrs Ivy Habershon OBE. J. P. A member of one of Rotherham's leading industrial families and a former Mayoress. She was born in India in 1892 and died 15 August 1962 aged 70 years.

This garden is worth a visit, especially in autumn, when the leaves are changing colour. There are many specimen trees and the Acers are a wonderful sight.

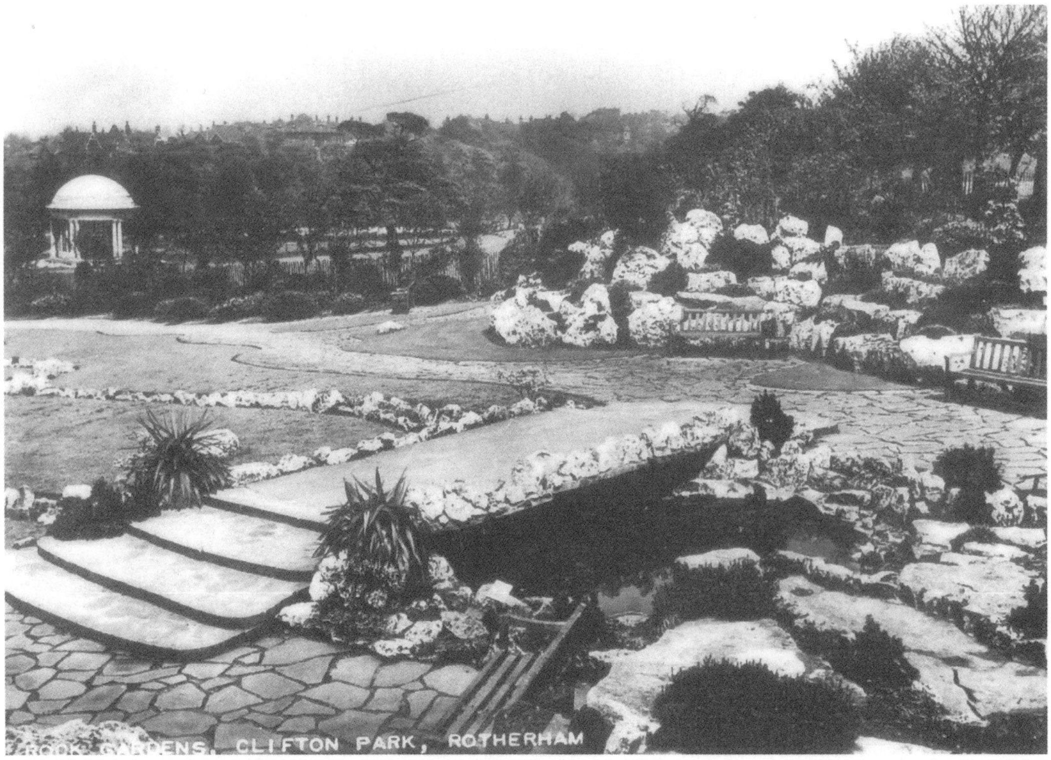


*Memorial Rock garden, 1952. (Rotherham Archives)*

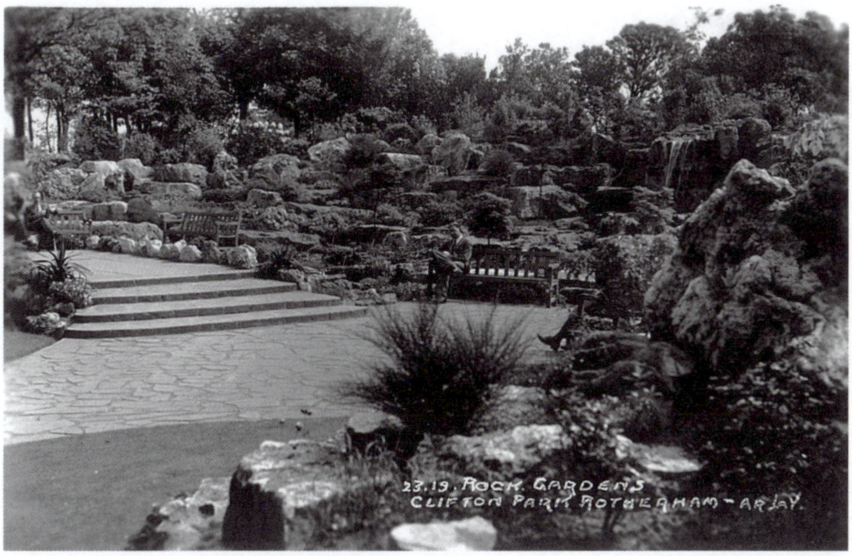


*Memorial Rock garden, 1952. (Author's postcard)*

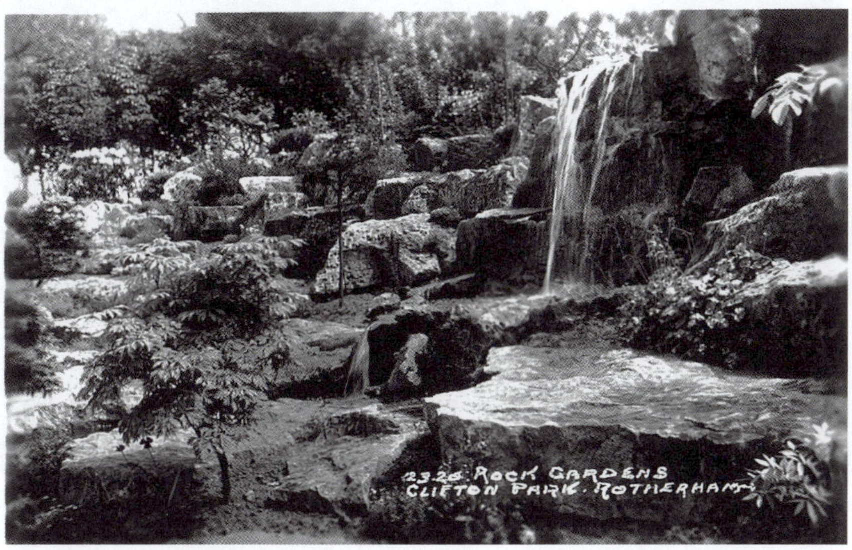


*Memorial Rock garden, 1957. (Author's postcard)*

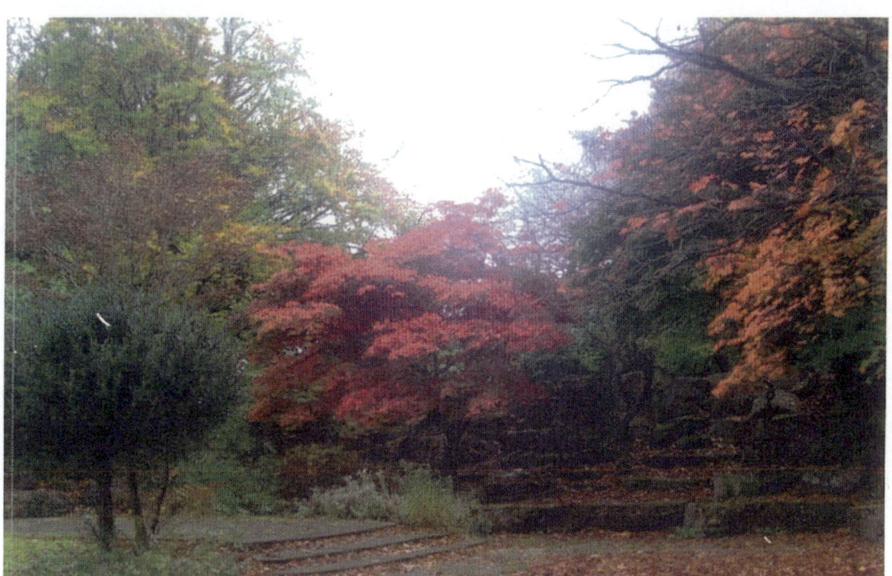

*Autumn colours in the Memorial Rock garden, 2008. (Author's photograph)*

# 14 WORLD WAR I CANNONS

In 1920's, three cannons given to Rotherham were displayed to the rear of the Museum.

The two smaller Victorian naval guns were given as a gift to the town from T.W. Ward of Sheffield, who had been breaking up an 'old man of war'. They were displayed either side of a large captured German naval gun made by Krupps. It was given to the town by the Government in 1921 in recognition of the efforts of the townspeople of Rotherham made for Britain during the Great War of 1914 – 1918.

The Council resolved to remove them in 1937 and they were scrapped in the local furnaces.

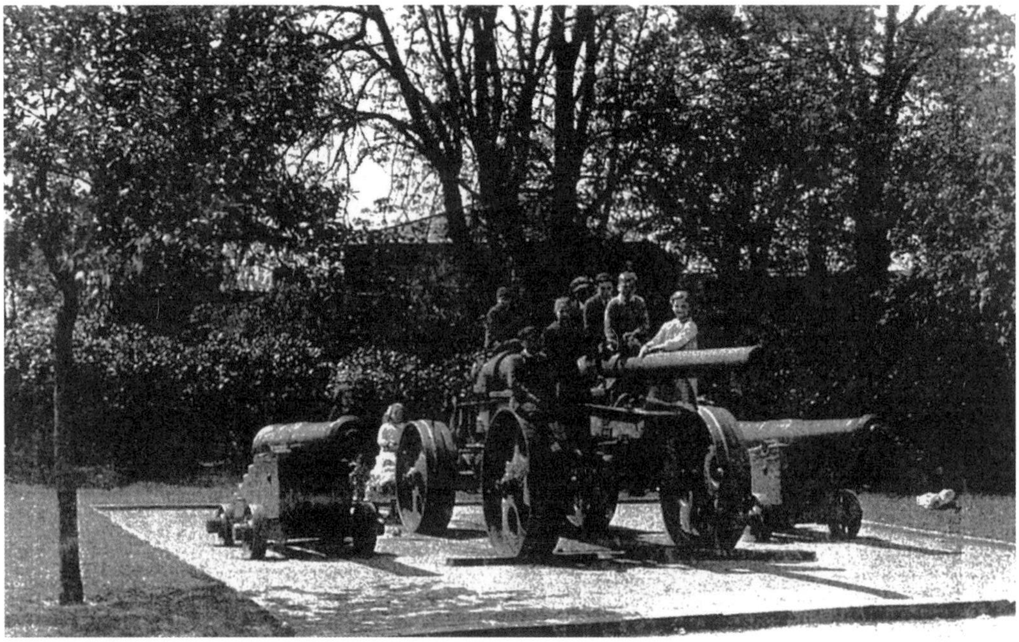

*Guns presented to Rotherham following The Great War. (Rotherham Archives)*

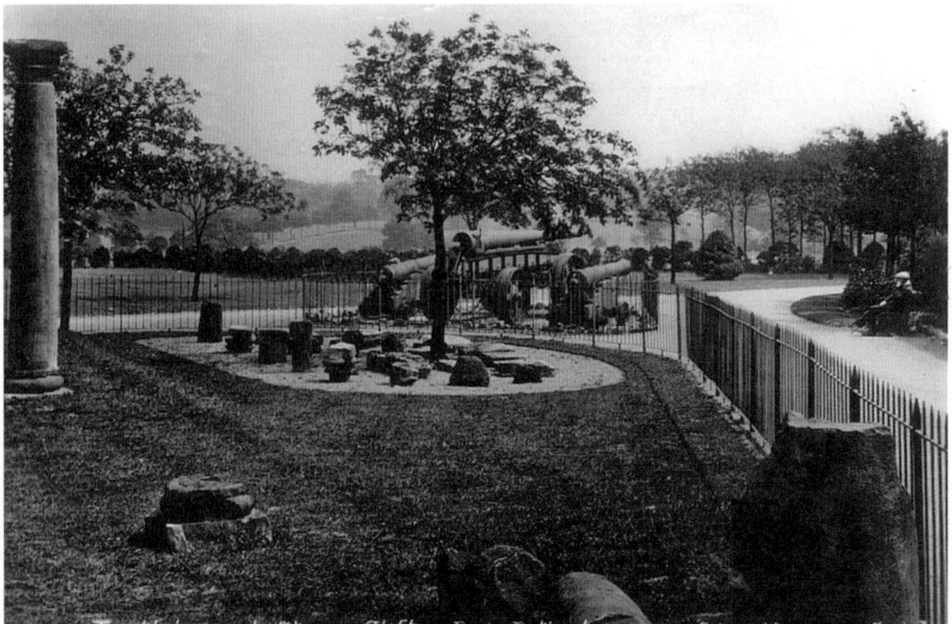


*Cannons near the granary. (Author's postcard)*

## 15 CLIFTON PARK TANK

In June1919, a British tank entered Clifton Park at the Bird Cage Lodge entrance and made its way to the Bandstand site the Mayor christened the tank 'Princess Mary'. The following year Big Willie's' WW1 tank was installed on the base of the old Bandstand and enclosed with railing. It was used in the Great War, fighting on the Somme, a Mark 5 composite tank of the 12th Battalion Tanks Corp, and presented in recognition of the town's contribution to World War 1.

Broken up in 1927, the proceeds from the sale of the scrap were donated to Military charities, namely £30 to St. Dunstan's and £30 to the Lord Kitchener's home.

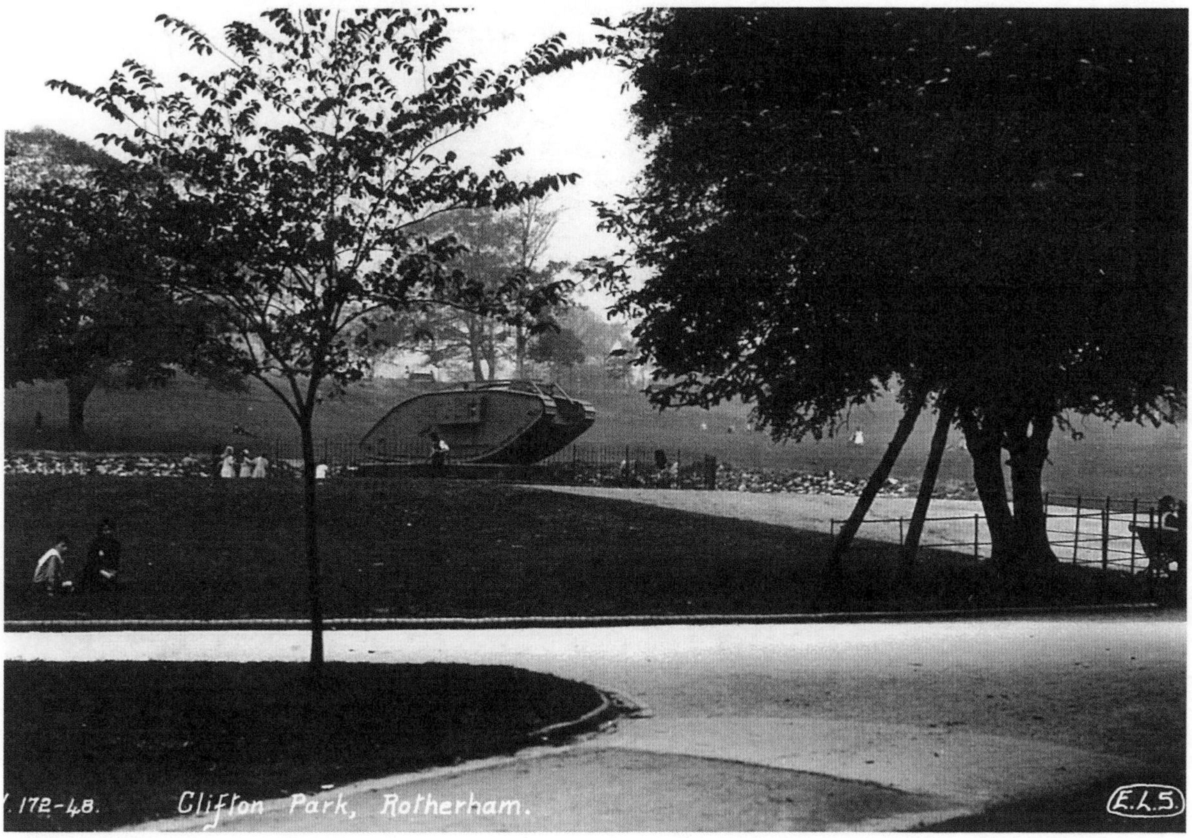


*Tank, 1919 - 1925*
*On the base of the original bandstand. (Author's postcard)*

## 16 THE TOWN STOCKS

In the 16th century, Rotherham Town Stocks were near to the Old Market Place and later transferred to the Parish Church. (Minster) The ancient stocks were found by workmen when excavations were underway at the original site of the White Hart Hotel, situated at the bottom of the church steps.

To the end of 1909, the Borough Engineer was authorised to place the one remaining part of the stocks in Clifton Park. Now to be found near the Roman Granary, to the rear of the Museum.

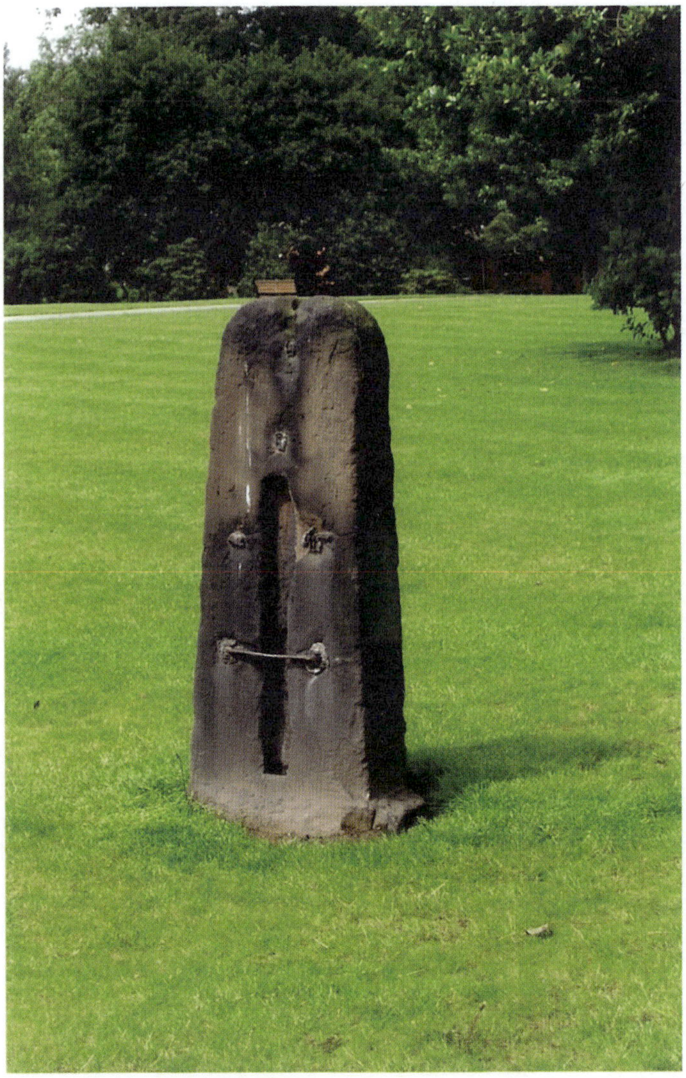

*Part of the town stocks transferred to the park from below the Parish Church steps. (Author's postcard)*

## 17 THE ROMAN GRANARY

The Roman Fort at Templeborough was excavated initially in 1877, however, very little was unearthed due to lack of funds.

At Steel, Peech and Tozers, on Sheffield Road, a new melting shop was required due to the demand for steel during the First World War. The Roman Fort site was requested.

The Borough Council employed Thomas May to excavate the fort, thought to be called Mobium, between November 1916 and July 1917.

The original stone columns from the Roman granary at Templeborough Fort were re-erected in Clifton Park, 1922. The Granary of the fort was transferred to the garden to the East of Clifton House as these remains were considered to be part of the Museum's collection of Roman artefacts in 1925.

Since that time there has been other finds around the edges of the site at Templeborough, but the fort remained sealed beneath the steelworks.

In 2006 and 2007, the works were demolished. Excavations began again but they revealed very little to add to the discoveries of Thomas May. Other finds have been discovered in the same vicinity; the fort's west road leading in the direction of Tinsley was made during the preparation of the site for the Brinsworth Strip Mill.

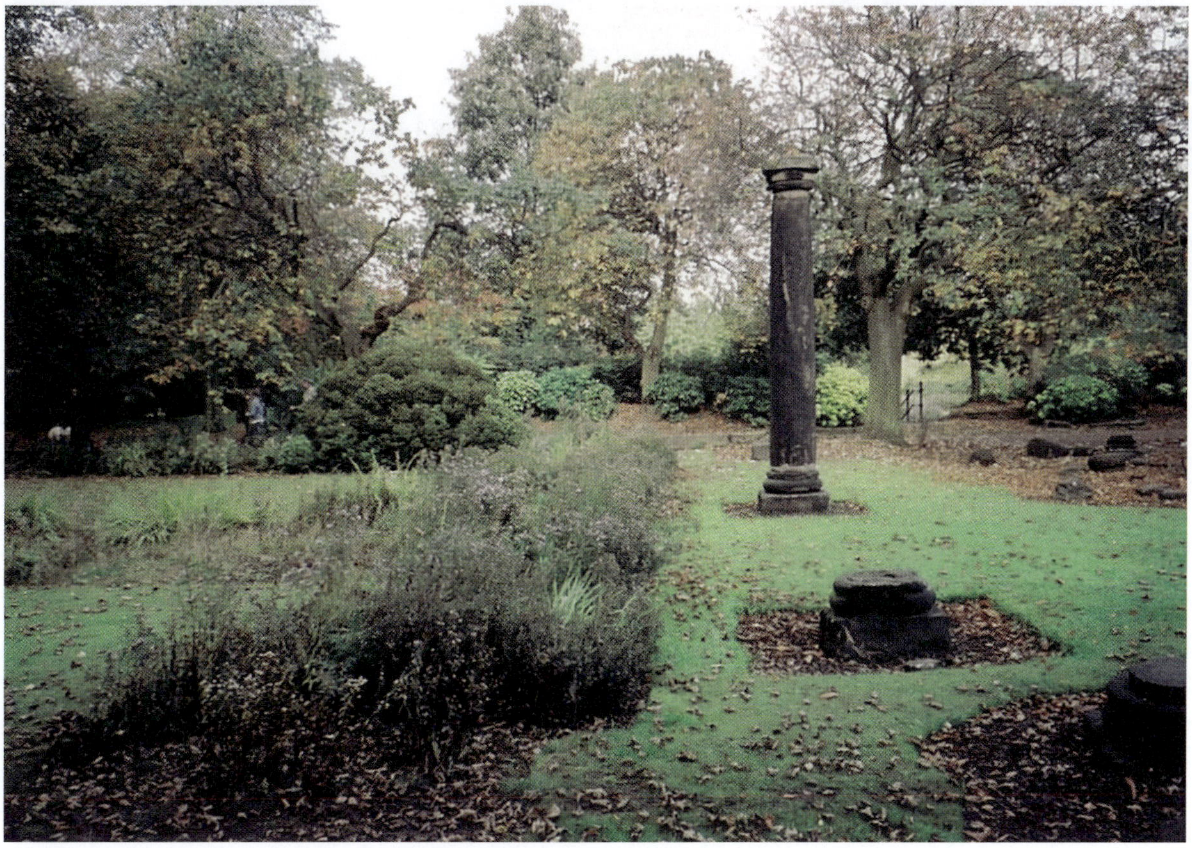

*The Roman Granary before restoration. (Author's photograph)*

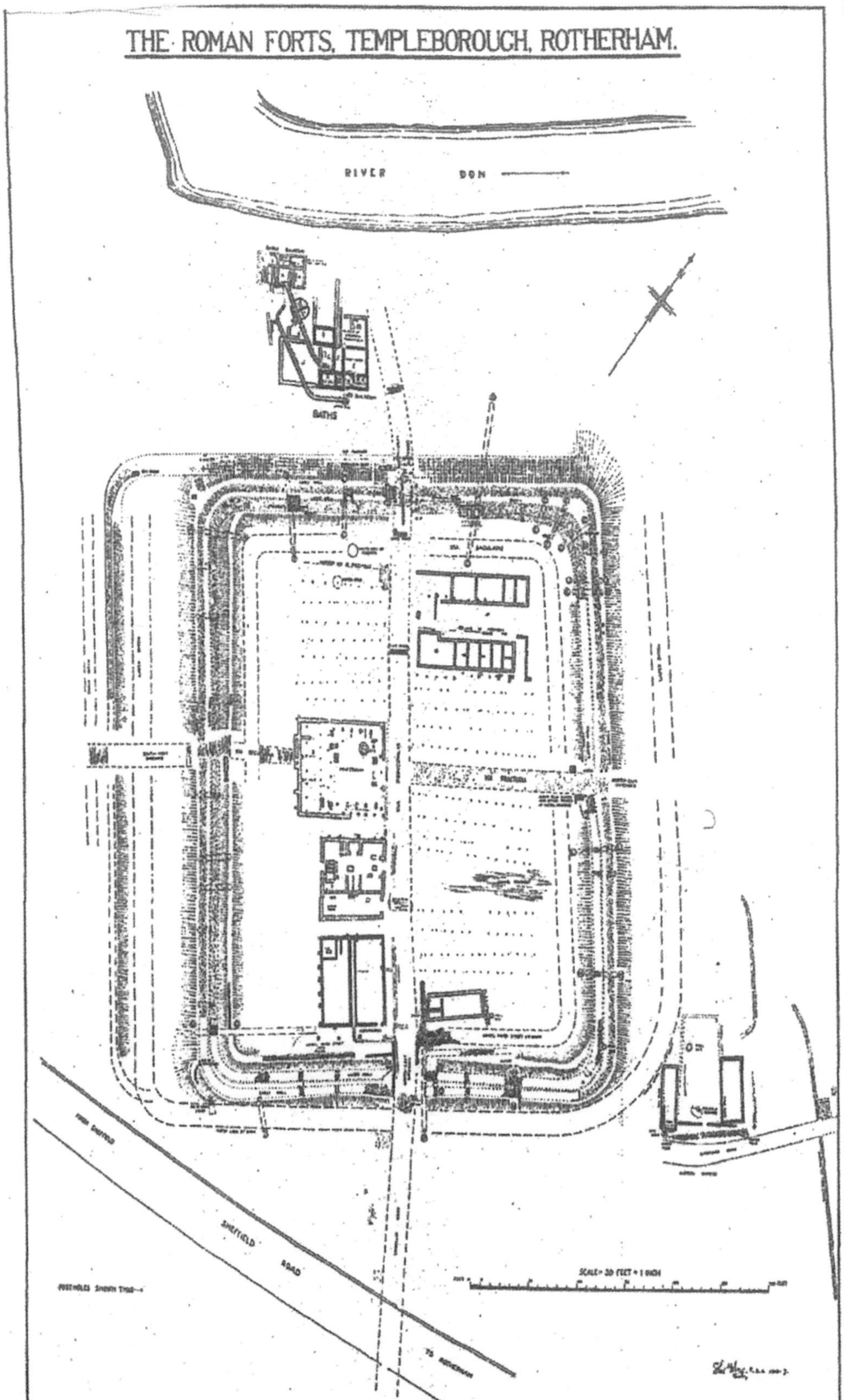


5 The full plan of the three fonts on the site was revealed by Thomas May's excavation of 1916-7. The original wood and earth fort had been rebuilt in stone around A.D. 100 and hastily rebuilt in the fourth century. May's excavation took place just before the site disappeared beneath Steel, Peech and Tozer's Templeborough Melting Shop in 1917. [May, T., *The Roman forts of Templeborough near Rotherham* (1922)]

# 18 THE SUNKEN GARDEN

In 1936, a garden was designed projecting into the parkland opposite the Roman Granary remains. It seemed to be a strange addition to have at that time; it probably compensates for the loss of flowerbeds where the Granary stands.

Known as the Sunken Garden or Rose Garden, it proved a quiet place to sit among the sweet smelling flowers. Surrounded by shrubs and hidden away down shallow steps and an entrance gate, the central feature was a drinking fountain. On the sweeping lawn to the rear of the Sunken Garden was a very high flagpole.

Plaques in Braille for blind people were placed around the park leading to the Sunken Garden in 1954.

The drinking fountain was removed and in the 1970s and the Walker sundial was put in its place.

In the 1990's, the garden was given another makeover. Sweet smelling plants, especially lavender, were used so it became a sensory maze.

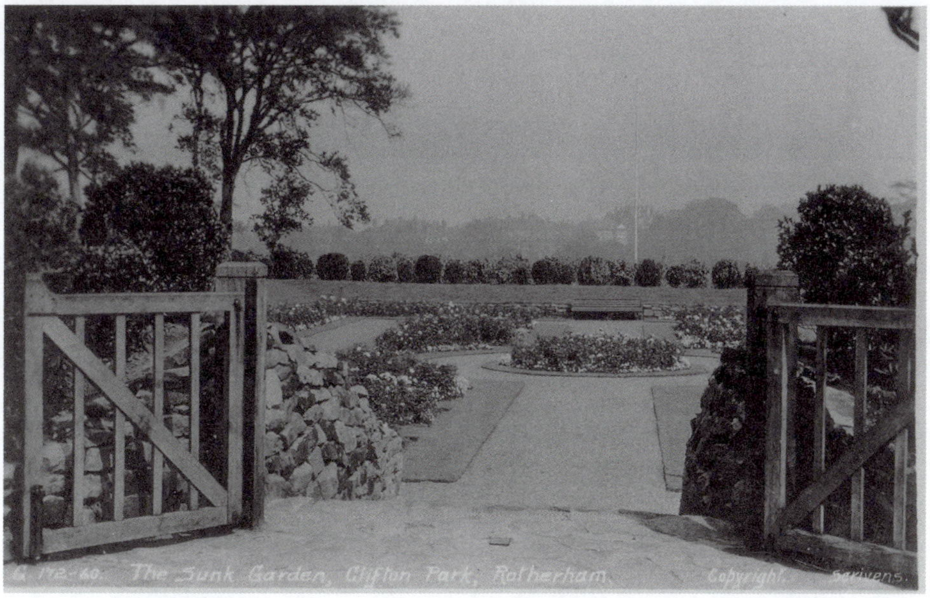


*The houses of Doncaster Road are seen in the background. Sunken garden. (Rotherham Archives)*

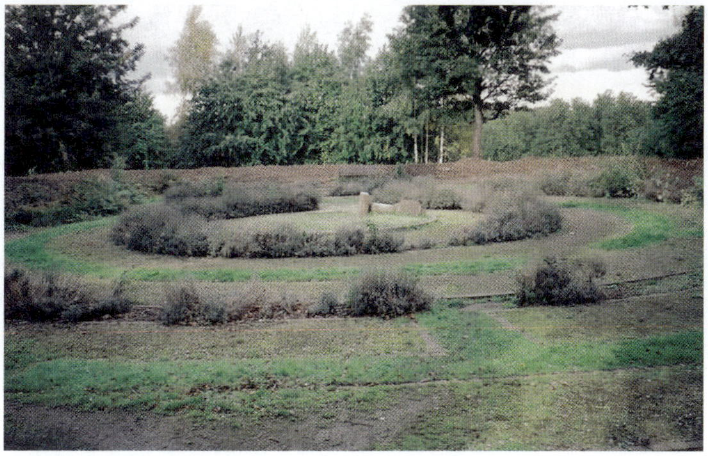

*Sunken garden in 2008 before it's removal showing the Walker sundial broken. (Author's photograph)*

## 19 THE BANDSTAND

A site near the lake was chosen for the first Bandstand that was manufactured in cast iron, it was a very intricate design. The local firm of Yates and Haywood made the railings around it. It is interesting to note that in May 1893, the Corporation stated that the Bandstand had to be finished in three weeks, failing that, they would complete it and make the contractor liable!

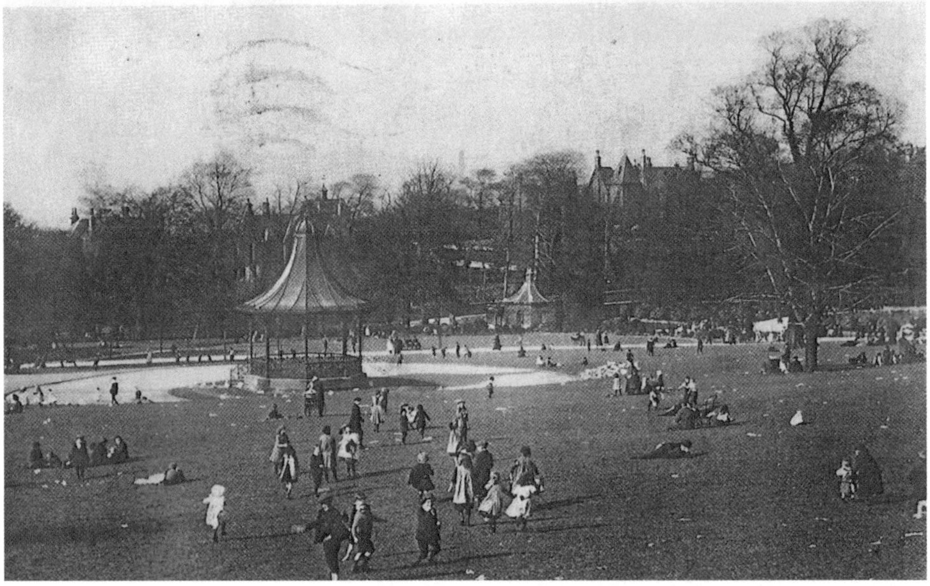

*Original bandstand, early 1900's. (Rotherham Archives)*

It opened in 1894 and was clearly visible from the dining room window of Clifton House.

In the 'IVANHOE REVIEW', September 1898, 'Janus' says, "Charles Elsom, who was the bandmaster of the Rotherham Borough Temperance Band and cornet player, played a variety of music for adults and children to dance to well into the evening."

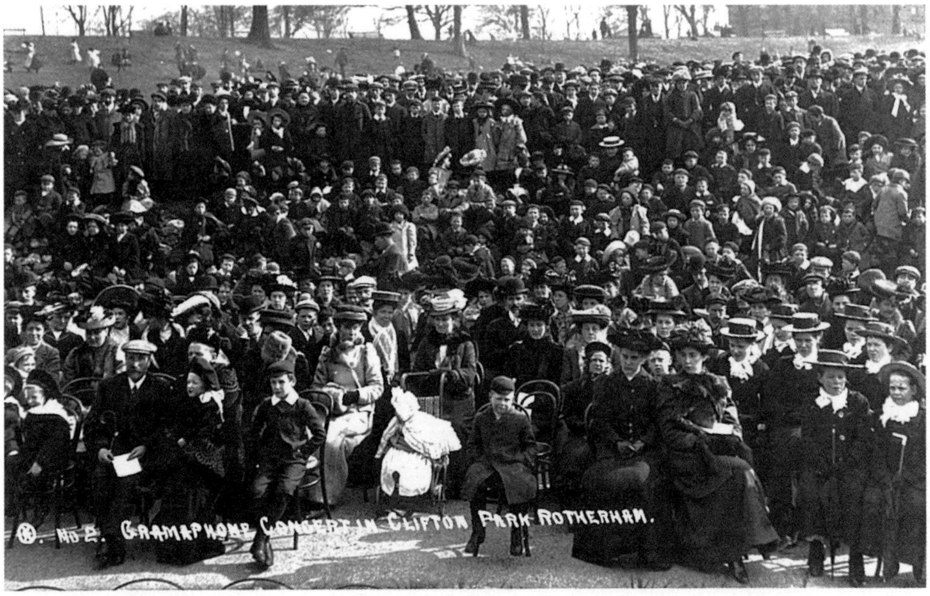


*Gramophone concert at the bandstand. Notice the Museum and a scarcity of trees. (Author's postcard)*

Other events ranged from the Eastwood Minstrels Band to gramophone concerts. An Auxetophone (an early compressed air gramophone designed by the British engineer Sir Charles Parsons) was used for the gramophone concerts. The amplification of sound made by compressed air pressed through the horn of the gramophone.

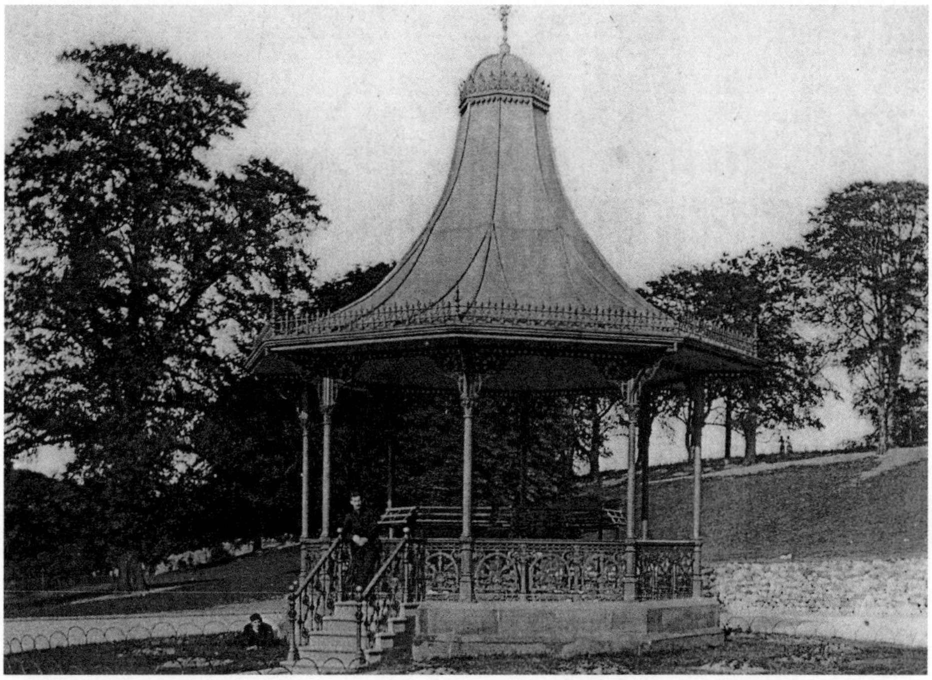

*The original bandstand which was moved to Masbro' recreational ground. (Rotherham Archives)*

Electric lamps were installed in 1911. Come 1919, the iron superstructure of the bandstand was removed and re-erected at Masborough Recreational Ground, known as Ferham Park now. A temporary Bandstand was erected near the Tank, Clifton Park, in May 1922.

The present day Bandstand was built by George Saul and Sons Limited, at the cost of £1,660 and opened 26th May, 1928 by the Mayor, Alderman W. Brooke.

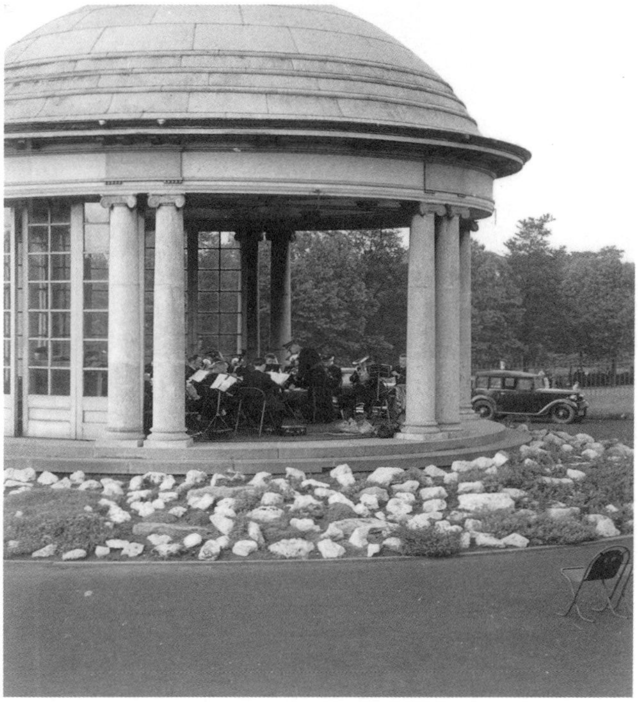

*Bandstand 1950's. (Rotherham Family History Society)*

It was an impressive sight; the pillars supported a copper dome, curved sliding doors offered protection against the wind, surrounded by a rockery and seating. The public paid to use a seat in the enclosed area, or sat around on the hillside listening to the bands. Across the path from the Bandstand was an ice cream kiosk so you could eat ice cream whilst enjoying the entertainment. Eventually the sliding doors were removed.

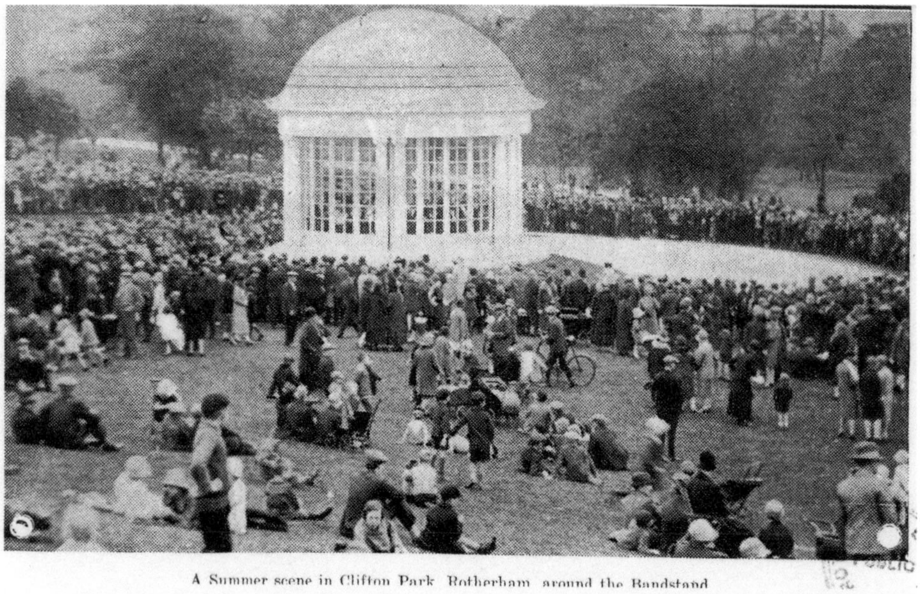


*A summer scene around the bandstand 1928. (Rotherham Archives)*

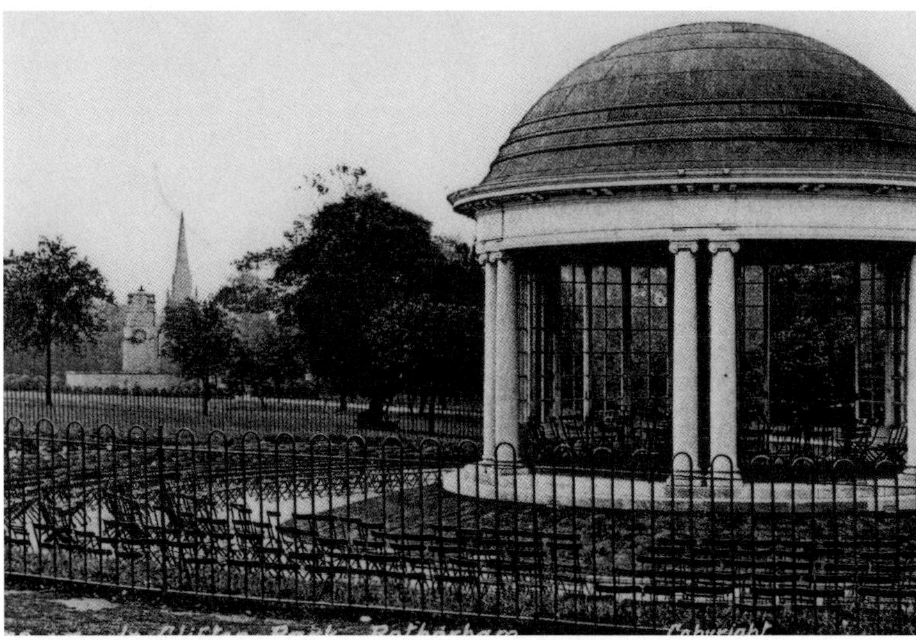

*Bandstand 1940's. Showing Cenotaph and Rotherham Parish Church in the background. (Rotherham Archives)*

In 1991, it was refurbished to mark the park's centenary. Her majesty, Queen Elizabeth II visited the park on this occasion and planted a tree nearby.

Many bands have played at the Bandstand. In 1901, a park band committee was formed to organise them:

Rotherham Volunteer Band
Rotherham Borough Band
Hallamshire Rivals Band
Yorkshire Dragoons Band
H.M. Royal Marine Band
York and Lancaster Band
And many more including:-

June 1911, at the Coronation of King George V, the Yorkshire Dragoons and in September 1912, The Sailor's Orphan Boys Brass and Reed Band

In 1914, bands played on Thursday evening from 7.15pm until 9.15pm – they were paid £4-10-0d for a two hour performance. An afternoon performance in the summer time could be anything up to £35.

Collecting sheets were placed at the entrance gates and a charge of 2d was made, and 3d for a reserved seat with a programme.

Various organisations used the Bandstand too, such as the Gloop's concerts and Band of Hope concerts.

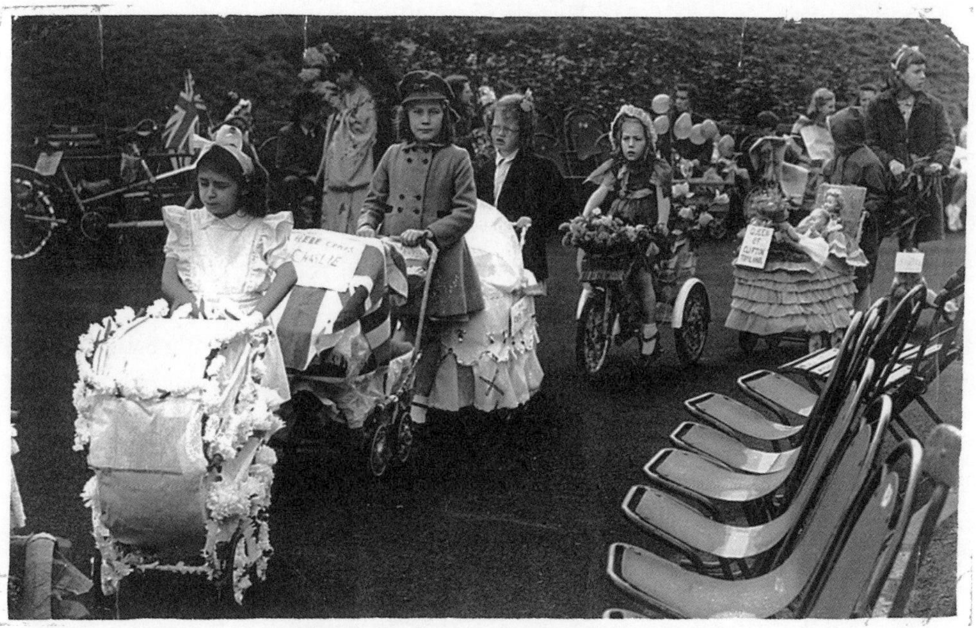

*Celebration of Prince Charles birth at the bandstand. (Author's photograph)*
*Note the author pushing the pram 3rd from the left*

## 20 WHIT WALKS

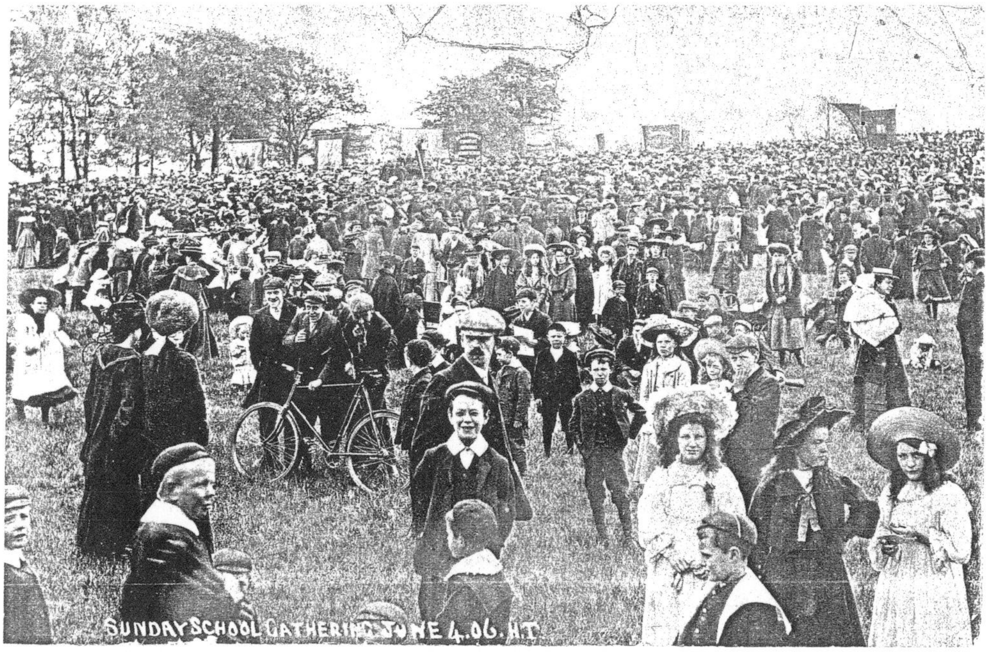


*Sunday school gathering. June 4th 1906, around the bandstand area. (Author's photograph)*

The Rotherham and District Sunday School Union Whit Walks began in 1905.

Each Whit Monday, every church and other places of Worship within the Rotherham boundary assembled at the site of the Rotherham Statutes fairground, now the Rotherham Police Station, and slowly paraded through the town and into Clifton Park. The route to the park passed Doncaster Gate Hospital where the staff pushed the patient's beds and wheelchairs outside to view the colourful spectacle.

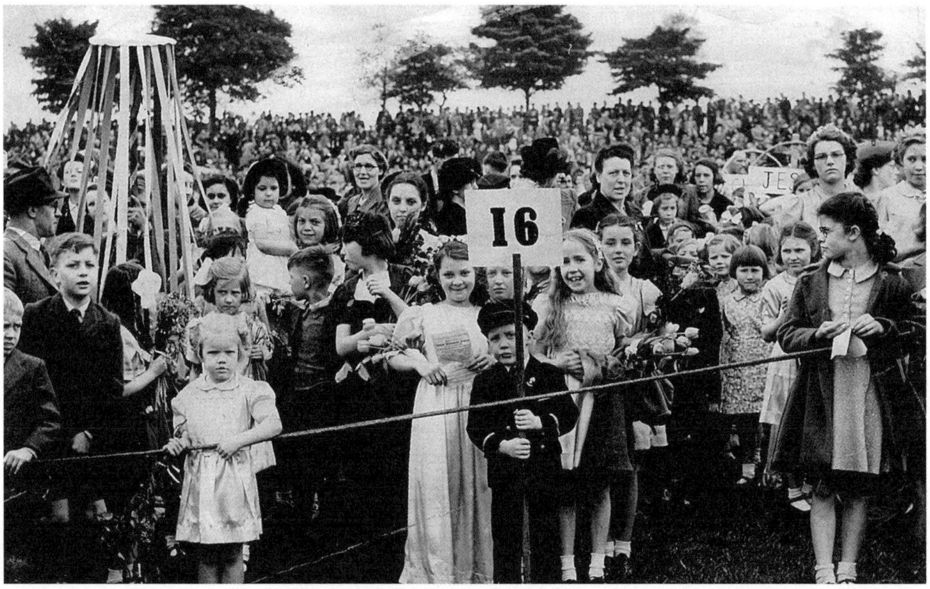


*Whit walk 1945. Barbara Cooke and Lillian Wright walk with Eastwood Church. (Barbara Cooke)*

Each Sunday school had a Queen or Captain with attendants and often accompanied by a brass band. A lorry was hired and decorated in the biblical theme of the year. With the stage set, the children dressed up to portray the characters of the story and proudly took their place on top of the lorry in the procession. The streets were lined with people watching the parade; they then followed it all the way up to Clifton Park and spent the rest of the day there.

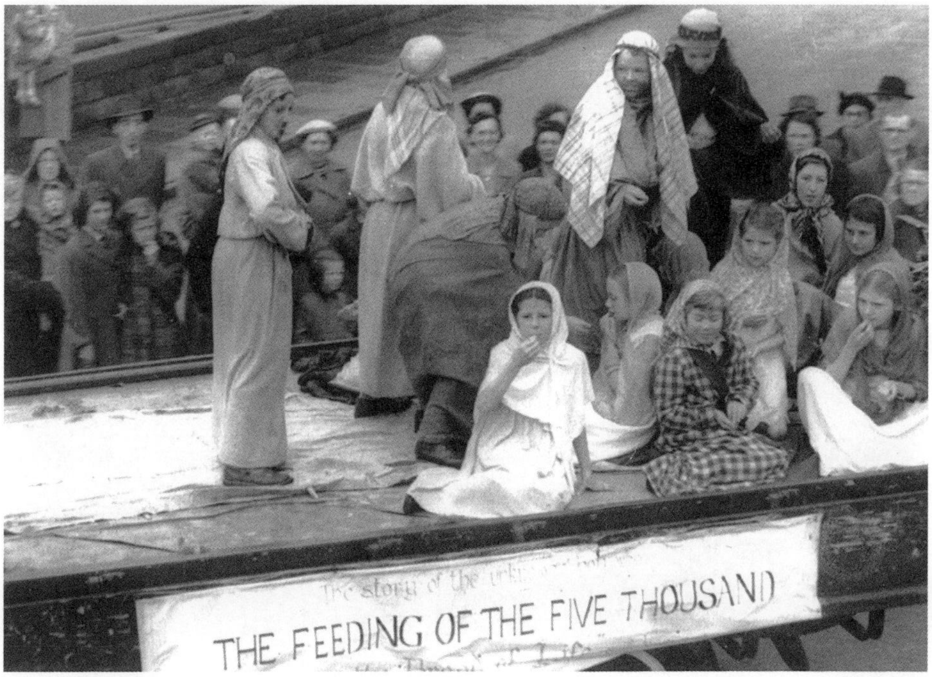


*Whit walk Sunday school float, 1950's. (Undisclosed)*

When the parade reached the Bandstand, with Sunday school banners waving, the best float and Sunday school was selected and duly presented with a cup by the Mayor and Mayoress. A short religious service followed.

Thousands of people crowded around the park and the Bandstand on Whit Monday. It was the day that all young people had their new 'Whitsuntide clothes' on and enjoyed showing them to all their friends.

Advertiser, 25 May 1907

*The cold morning of Whit Monday told against a bright display on the occasion of the third festival arranged in conjunction with the Rotherham and District Sunday School Union. Many of the children appeared in the procession wearing coats and jackets to protect them from the chill wind, consequently the pretty effect that is obtained by light dresses and coloured ribbons was lost.*

## 21 TREES

Clifton Park is an urban park, it is important because of the many varieties of trees and grassland; it also supports a range of wildlife and birds.

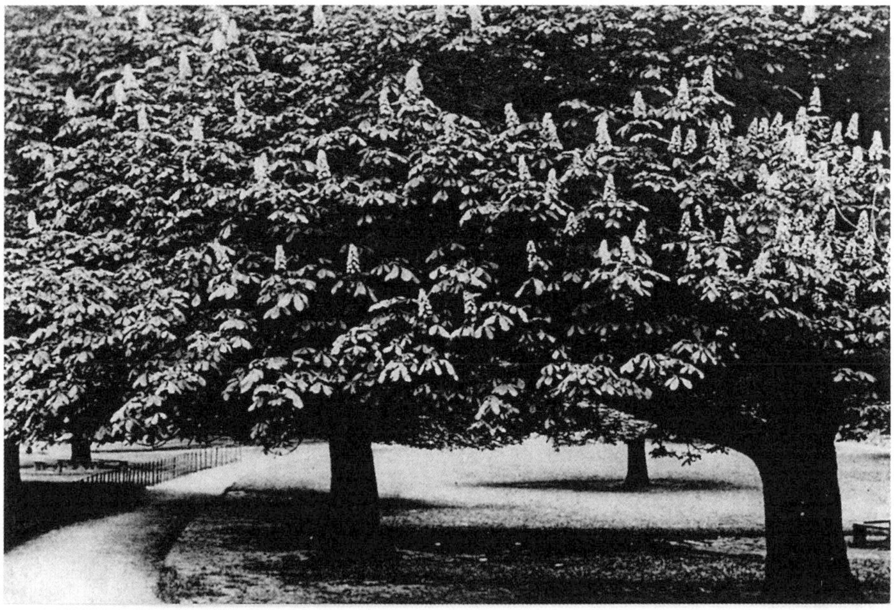

*Chestnut walk 1902 - 1915. Leading from the main pathway to the Bird Cage Lodge entrance. (Rotherham Archives)*

The Walker family, after purchasing the land, chose to plant up the boundaries with trees whose leaves were differently coloured and at that time, these were hardly used and very rare. Horse Chestnuts were very expensive and often only used in pleasure gardens, not parks, but the Sweet Chestnut was very popular largely for its timber value.

The Oak and Sweet Chestnut were used for fencing, gateposts and boats as they withstood harsh weather conditions.

Other trees were scarce, but a tree group remains in Clifton Park that is thought to have provided shelter for the animals.

The old Beech tree near to the Memorial Garden, planted around 1838 to mark the coronation of Queen Victoria, making it approximately 177 years old. In 1959, the lower branches were suspended by cables to the higher branches because of the strain caused by the boys playing Tarzan on them! A number of branches have broken away from the main trunk. The life of a Beech tree is around 200 years; this tree will be so sadly missed when it finally dies and disappears. So many people when asked about Clifton Park mention the Beech tree, speaking fondly of it. The tree came under threat again in 2000 when a branch broke away. Fortunately, it was given a stay of execution after a thorough inspection. It was fenced off for safety reasons.

To the rear of the Beech tree is a Horse Chestnut, thought to be approximately the same age.

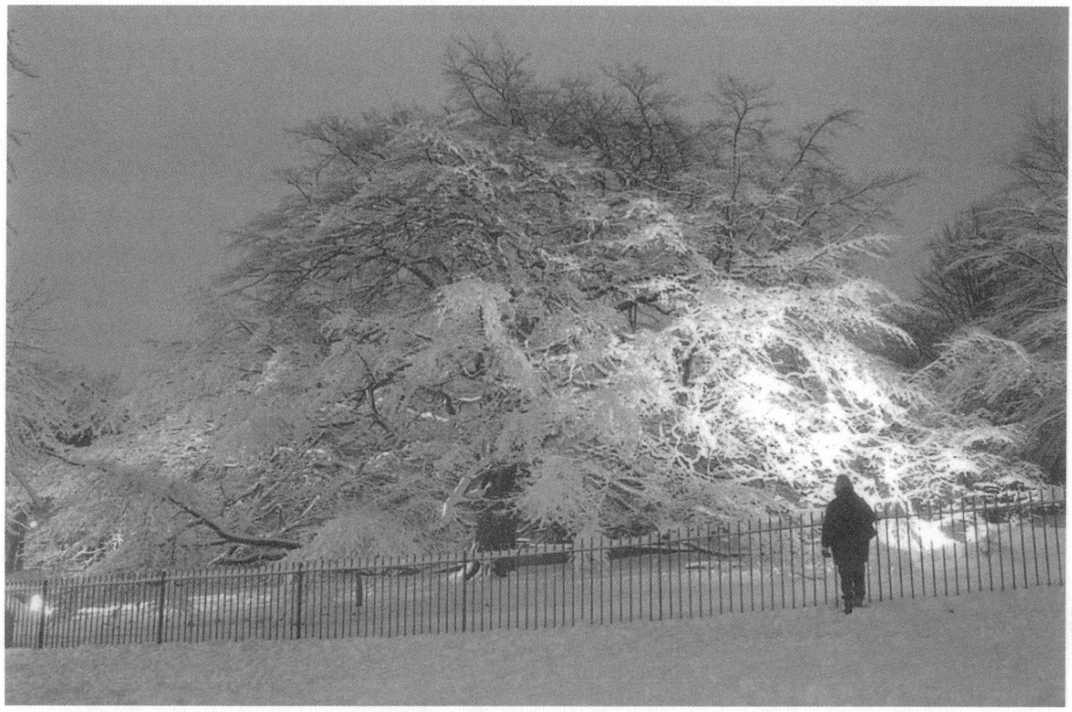

*The Beech Tree illuminated on a winters night. (Rotherham Family History Society)*

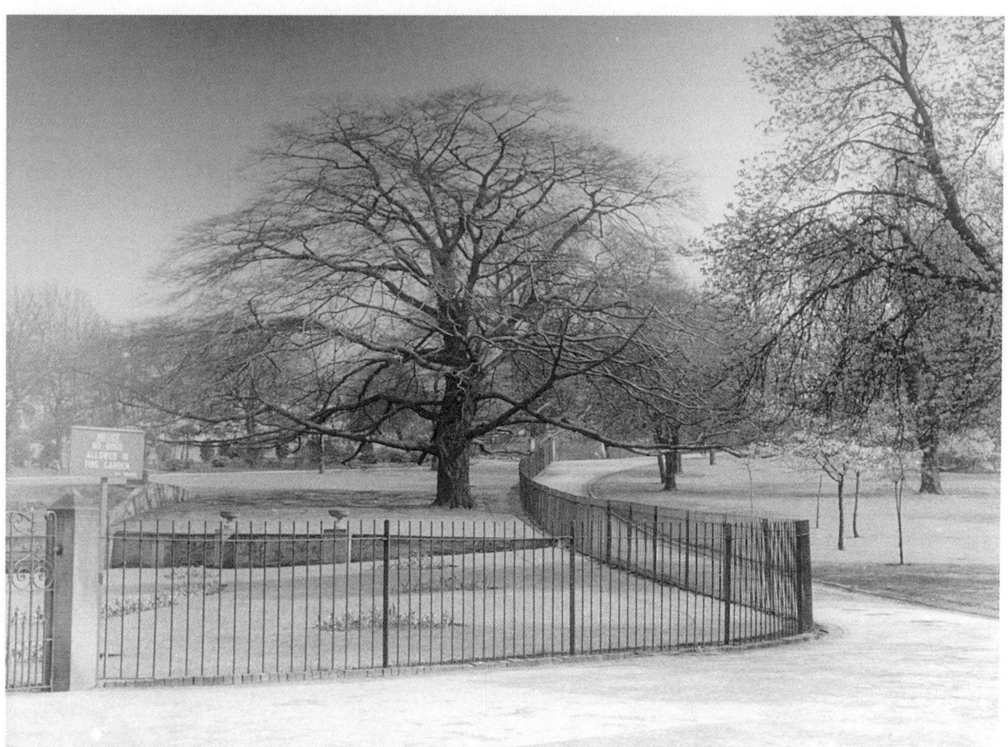

*The Beech Tree with memorial garden in the foreground, 1950's. (Rotherham Family History Society)*

When new walkways were made in 1891, one hundred each of Chestnut, Lime and Elm were planted along them. The people of Rotherham donated many trees. Mr J Lister, of Listerdale, gave a gift of young trees from his own woodland.

In 1903, thirty-three Red Chestnut trees were removed from Boston Park and taken to Clifton Park; it said they were pushed on wheelbarrows! By 1904, many of the young Elms were diseased, these and other dead trees, were cut down and burnt.

A report by Mr. W. Dallimore of Kew Gardens in 1909 stated:
*That the mortality of the old trees is due entirely to a bad atmosphere, caused by smoke and other impurities, and it is doubtful whether anything can be done to permanently benefit the remaining old trees whilst the present atmospheric conditions prevail.*

Recommendations were given for the planting of new trees. Baedeker's Great Britain Guide book also referred to Rotherham as 'a smoky, iron-working town of 42,000 inhabitants. Indeed, the Yorkshire colliery belt was becoming so bad that evergreens could not survive in peoples' gardens and parks.

Pollutions, weather and disease has been the main reason that many trees have been lost over the last 100 years. It is noted that in 1911 and 1937, the Mayor and members of the corporation planted tress to celebrate the Coronation Years. A tree nursery in Clifton Park grew trees for the whole of Rotherham in 1914.

March 1914, dead trees were felled, sent to the sawmills and made into railings. On the main walk and as far as the Middleton Road entrance, London Plane, Sycamore and Wheatley Elms were planted.
Between 1922 and 1939, 250 dead trees were removed and there was nothing to replace them, but in post-war years, there had been a gradual reduction in pollution and big planting schemes were commenced.

Gales in 1962 caused many trees to be lost and in December 1982, 200 mature Elms were lost due to Dutch Elm disease. It rampaged throughout the country and in Clifton Park, 25% of the tree stock was lost, which included the avenue of Elms on the main pathway from the Middle Lane entrance. These trees had withstood 100 years of pollution and were an enormous loss to the park. The Elms were replaced by many other native trees, all of them being appropriate to a park of this age.

A weeping ash and beautiful turkey oaks are to be seen in the park and along the main pathway to the Cenotaph; London Plane trees stand majestically on either side.

The species Metasequoia (Dawn Redwood) was first discovered in 1941 in the grounds of a Chinese Temple; by 1948, these trees had arrived in England. There are six in Clifton Park, now standing over 60 feet tall and can grow to 100 feet, so they have yet to reach their full maturity. The foliage is pale green in summer, turning orange in the autumn before shedding its needles.

Around the park are special trees planted for celebrations and memorials.

In the 1990's, the park was heavily planted resulting in the loss of visual connections between the park and the museum, however, when the trees are in full leaf they do hide Rotherham's only high rise flats. Ariel views show the tree cover is very dense in places, a vast difference from 100 years ago.

In 1991, Queen Elizabeth II planted a tree opposite the Bandstand to mark the park's centenary. October 2005, the Mayor, Councillor Hilda Jacks, to mark 200 years since the battle of Trafalgar, planted a sturdy young oak tree. This should flourish by the side of the bandstand for many years.
A special civic visit took place to celebrate 10 years of the twinning of Rotherham with Riesa in Germany. As part of the 10th Anniversary celebration, a tree was planted in Clifton Park. The Mayor of Riesa gave this tree to the people of Rotherham in July 2007.

The rock garden is the place to visit to see many specimen trees, especially in autumn when the leaves are changing colour.

The Horse Chestnuts look wonderful too, but in the autumn, they must groan to each other when they see the annual pilgrimage of young people armed with sticks attempting to get their prized conkers! Horse Chestnuts line one of the pathways leading onto Doncaster Road, it is known as the Chestnut walk.

British Woodlands are more extensive today than they have been for centuries. Forest cover in the UK is approximately 8,893 square miles (11.8% of land). This has not been matched since the 1750's when forests were plundered to expand the Royal Navy's fleet as well as for charcoal to produce gunpowder.

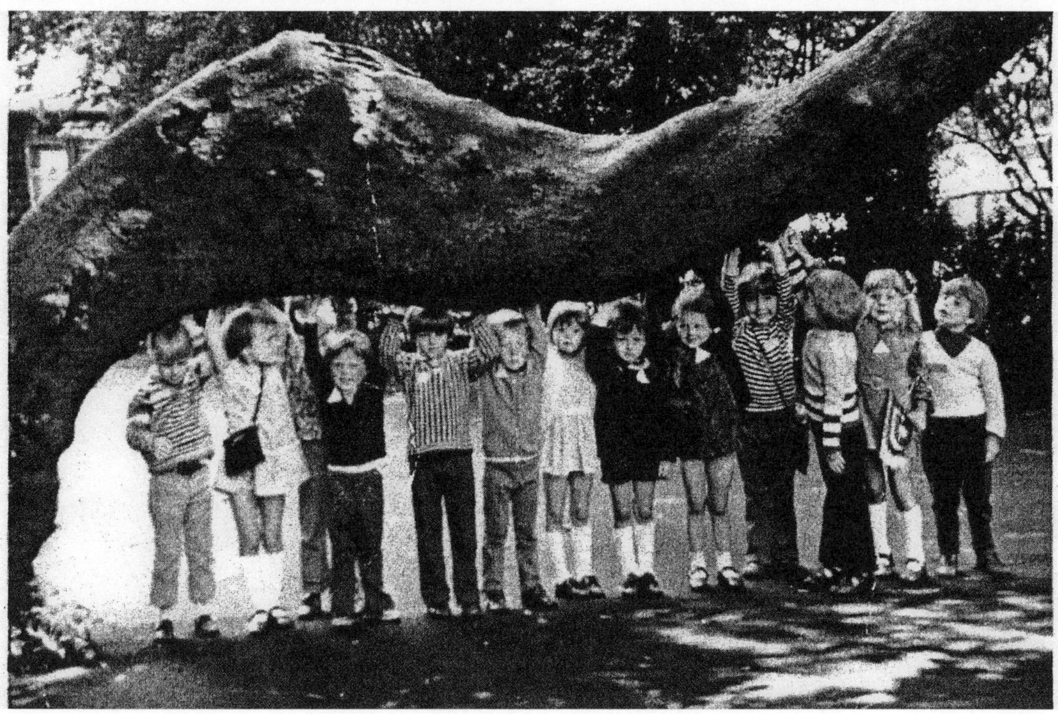

*Conisbrough children enjoying an outing to Clifton Park posing beneath the "Camel Tree". (Mr. Keith Butcher. Bygone Conisbrough and Denaby)*

In the 1940's and 1950's a special tree stood behind the children's amusements and near the donkeys. The trunk bent over resembling a camel's back and all children had great fun on it.

## 22 WILDLIFE

Since 1975, some 54 species of birds have been recorded in the park; tits, linnet, meadow pipit, redwing, bullfinch, greater spotted woodpecker, barn and tawny owl to name but a few. Some of these birds are now of conservation concern.

During a field survey in 2002, mistle thrush, redwing, nuthatch, goldfinch, goldcrest, blackbird, chaffinch and wren were among the species seen. There was no external evidence on the trees of bats, however, they can be seen flying around the park at dusk.

A bird called a white-faced whistler that died in the park in February 1902 was given to the Museum and an egg from one of the swans also given.

In 2007, the bird population was thriving, nearly all the bird boxes were occupied by the smaller species and many magpies, wood pigeons and collared doves also nesting in the park. Woodpeckers were seen in 2010.

Thirteen species of butterflies were recorded in 2001. Foxes can be seen regularly, as can the resident grey squirrels.

Schoolchildren often visit with their school for nature trails and are helped by the Rangers and museum staff. For members of the public, park trails are regularly held which cover various topics.

# 23 FLOWER BEDS

Clifton Park has always been noted for its beautiful floral displays.

The parks committee employed many apprentices who, in turn, assisted the regular staff and helped to design individual planting for important areas, managed the flowerbeds and gardens. The main flower display at the Rotherham Show was also the responsibility of the apprentices.

In 1922 at a cost of £100, heating equipment plus material from the greenhouse was transferred from Selwood House on Doncaster Road.

Plants were grown from seed at the main nursery and it was noted that on the 13th April 1938, that 'the pricking out of seedlings for the summer bedding was in full swing and already 24,000 had been pricked out'!

Each year, a special flowerbed was created inside the main park entrance and called the 'Apprentices Bed' by everyone.
Carpet bedding was very popular in parks and used to develop the apprentices skills, but it was very labour intensive and costly. Baden Powell Centenary and Robert Burns Bi-Centenary are just two of the flower beds which were planted.

In 1979 the Rotherham Coat of Arms was magnificent. Three gardeners, Dave Collumbine, Mark Smith and Anthony Booth took 13 days to prepare and plant this bed. Amongst the many plants used were Red Attenanthea, Echeveria and Golden Moss.

In 1991, a London based private contractor won a tender to maintain the parks and gardens and sadly, the condition of Clifton Park deteriorated. Fortunately, the maintenance contract was back in the control of Rotherham Metropolitan Borough Council in 2009 and the park has improved immensely.

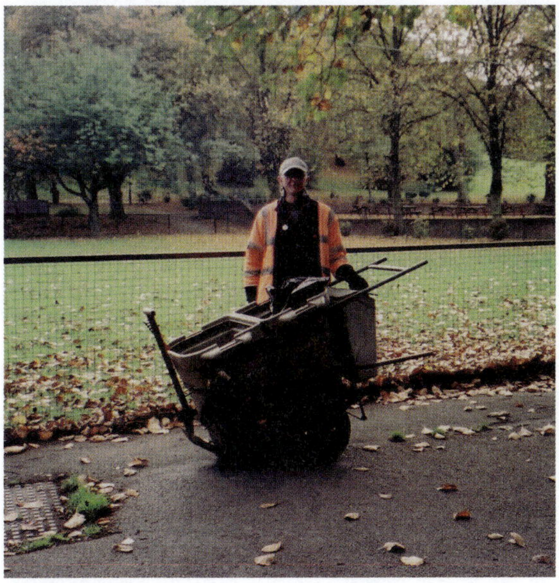

*Glen Ford. The fastest litter picker in Rotherham, 2007. (Author's photograph)*

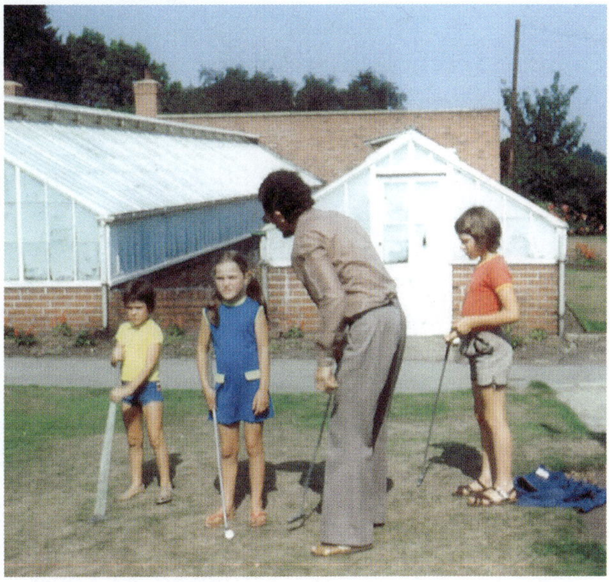

*Greenhouses at the edge of bowling greens and putting green. (Author's photograph)*

# 24 CRIME

Throughout its 124 years, Clifton Park has always experienced problems with unruly behaviour.

In 1905, there was unruly conduct by youths, trespassing especially at weekends and documents show that barbed wire was placed on the top of the Doncaster Road wall to keep them out.

During WW1, the park remained open during the night so munitions workers could cut through to work, this led to unseemly behaviour. A constable was employed to patrol the park, unfortunately, things did not improve. Rotherham Advertiser September 1917 reports, "*Young people wearing straw hats and gaudily looking shirts visited Clifton Park. They had foul mouths and low tastes and polluted the atmosphere with ribald and indecent remarks*!"

Police constables patrolled the park during the school holidays in 1916. 18th August 1919, Park Rangers were appointed and duly sworn in as police constables.

In 1922 a large amount of damage was done to walls and borders by hooligans.

In September 1935 new greenhouses were broken into and plants stolen.

In the 1950's, the park keeper was a formidable sight striding out around the park. He wore a blue uniform, peak cap and had a stick under his arm. Most children were afraid of him.

June 1997, hooligans wrenched a WW1 plaque that contained the names of the men from The York and Lancs Regiment from the curtain wall of the cenotaph. Fortunately, it was found on the ground just a few feet away.

The installation of CCTV near the children's play area in 1988 was not successful.

October 2002, an urban ranger service was introduced in Rotherham. Julian Mullins was appointed the first senior ranger with a staff of four based in Clifton Park; their duties took them to all the towns' green spaces. This was a very successful addition, greatly reassuring the general public. CCTV cameras were installed, this time successfully.

The Rangers worked with young people in the park, organising many activities during the school holidays and at weekends. They were also on hand to assist the park users with any untoward incidents.

Havelock Etches served in the Police Force until his retirement. He became a park keeper in Clifton Park

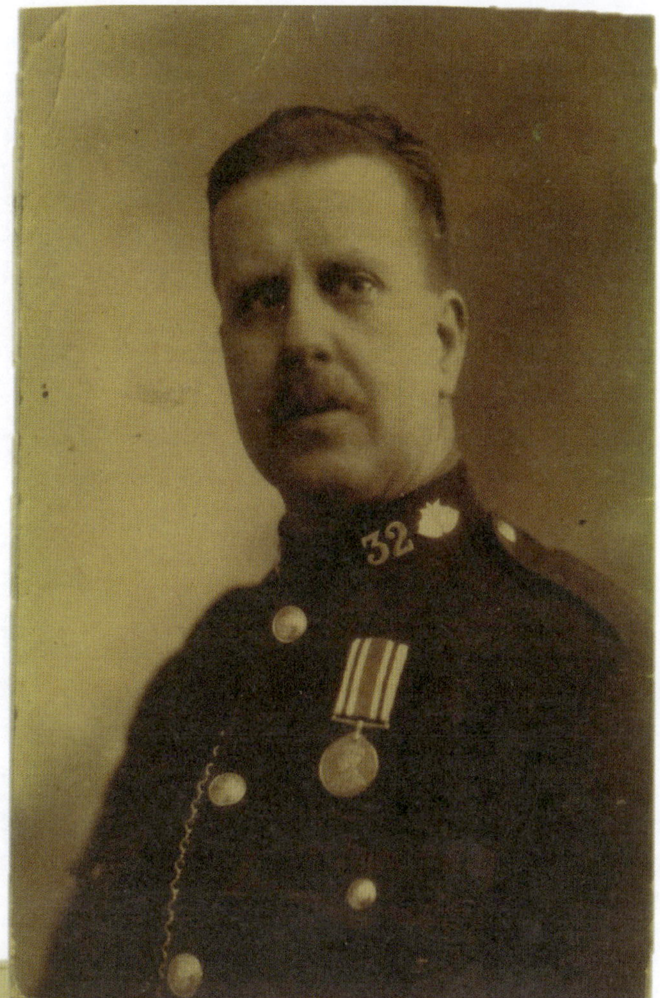


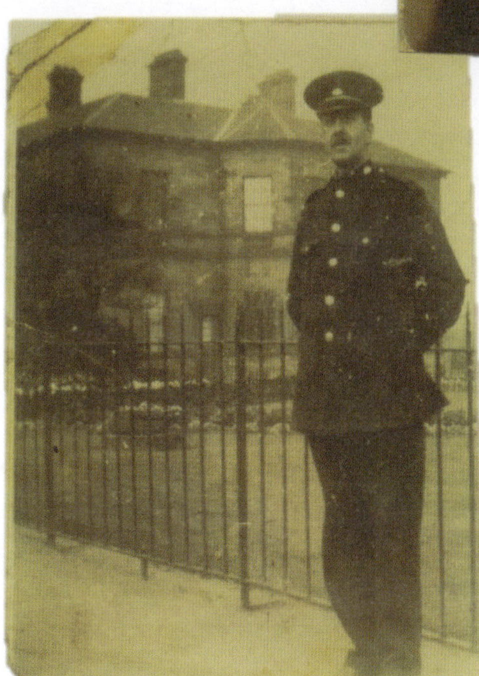

*(Author's postcards)*

# 25 THE WAR YEARS

## THE BOER WAR 1899-1902

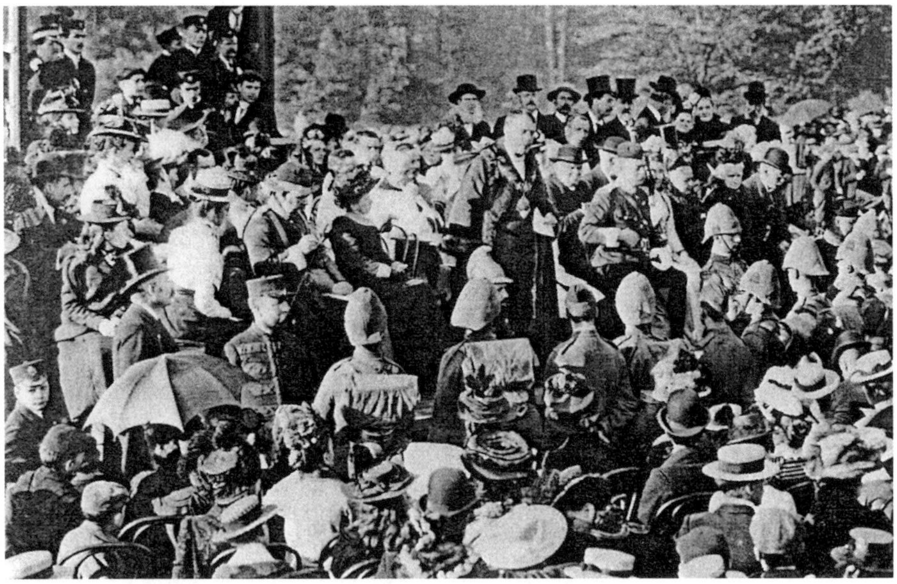

*Soldiers welcomed back to Rotherham from the Boer War, 1901. (Rotherham Archives)*

More than 55,000 British soldiers were wounded, captured or killed in the Boer War. Many were from the Rotherham area and lists of names can be found in the Rotherham Minster and local archives. 1901, Clifton Park welcomed home eight soldiers who had been fighting in the Boer War.

## THE GREAT WAR

November 1916 Rotherham townsfolk were invited to see a model dugout that was built; it was large enough to accommodate a large family. Wooden supports were used for the sides rather than sandbags. In the end, these were not necessary.

March 1918 a plane, taking part in a First World War air display, crash-landed in the park. Parts from the aeroplane were taken to 'Biggles' Restaurant, Swallownest, for a display.

There is an account in the Rotherham Advertiser dated 26 July 1919 of how the town celebrated peace after World War 1, *"The Peace celebrations began in the town and proceeded with a Mayoral parade into Clifton Park. The historic gathering of approx. 30,000 people began with a Drum Head Service. It was followed by flag displays, dancing, sports, Morris dancing. There was a large attendance at a boxing tournament which was held near the World War 1 Tank. There was dancing in the evening but the firework display was cancelled due to rain."*

## WORLD WAR II

When war was declared, a fete was in progress in Clifton Park and many people rushed home to listen to the news on the radio.

Rotherham had one of the lowest number of children evacuated from their homes and some who were only went as far as Kiveton Park. It is believed this was due to fathers being employed in the local steel factories or mines and family units were not disrupted.

Clifton Park adapted well and put to good use at this time. A surface shelter dug in September 1939 for protection of children, but never used. Flowerbeds became vegetable plots in 1941, potato and root crops followed in 1943.

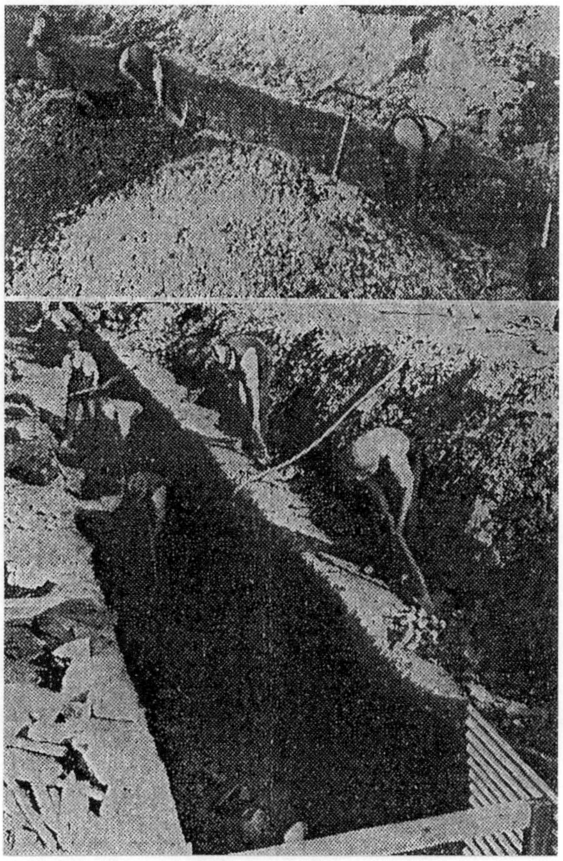

*Trench systems for shelter showing the considerable depth of the excavations. (Rotherham Advertiser)*

Although no evidence found, in the area of the park that borders Middleton Road, it is rumoured that the cabbage beds were stripped clean by a plague of rooks or rats!

Many park staff enlisted in 1940. In June of the same year, HM Forces based in Rotherham were granted free use of the park's sports facilities and at a Unity Demonstration sixty-one members elected to join the Home Guard.
The biggest blow to the people of Rotherham was the loss of the 50-year-old beautiful gates at the main entrance and all the iron fencing around the park. In 1941, they were given for the 'war effort', sadly not replaced.

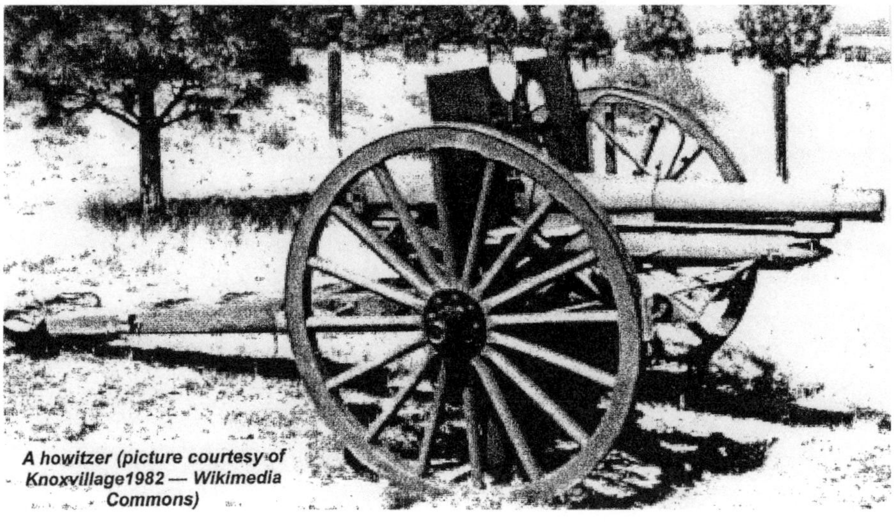


*World War I Howitzer*

Next to the scarp walk were water supply pipes that supplied the static water tanks. During snowy periods, children sledged over the path then the pipes on towards the bandstand. It was a bumpy ride and given the nickname, the 'rusty bump'.

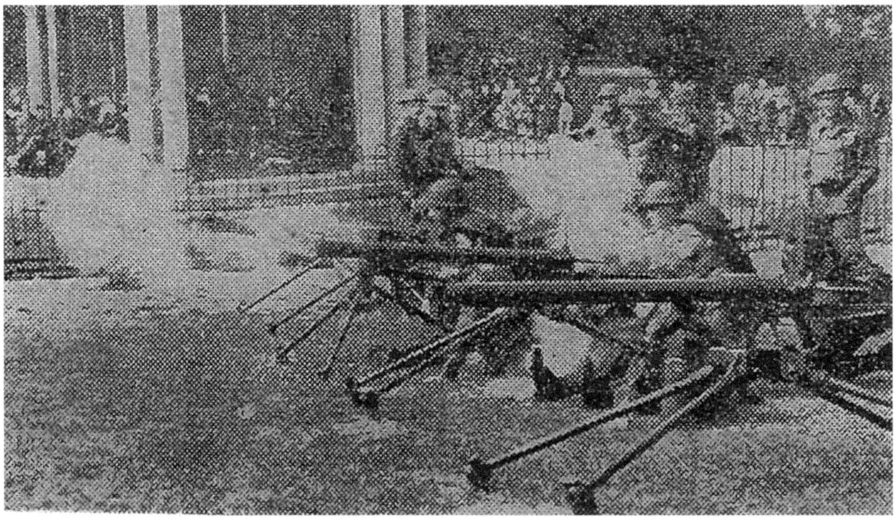

*Home Guard 1942. (Rotherham Advertiser)*

In September 1941 there was a tank parade through the town centre and park. A column of modern tanks comprising of 1 "Waltzing Matilda", 2 "Valentines" and 2 armoured cars. Accompanying them were a complement of 20 men; several had served in France and Libya. The tanks were on view to the public for three evenings; this was to boost the sale of War Bonds. From May of that year, Rotherham (Borough) Home Guard held exercises in the park.

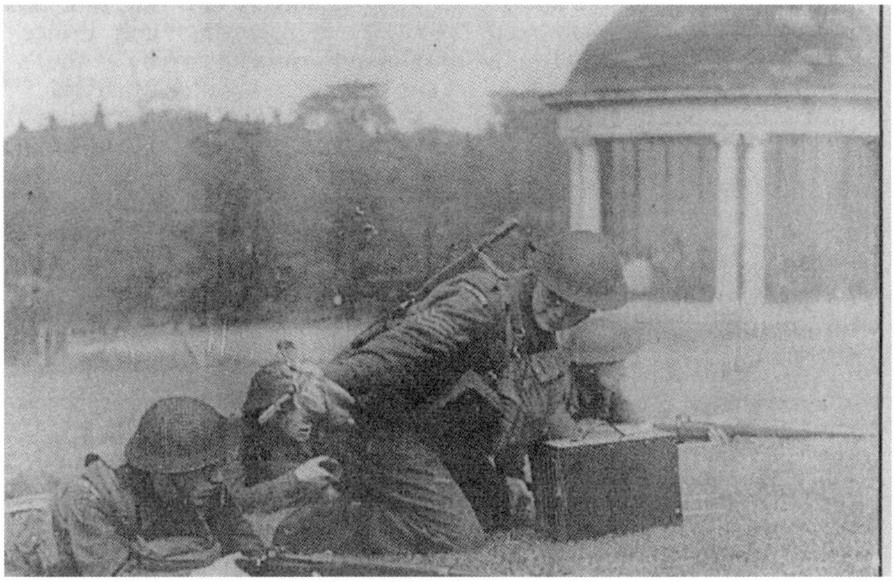

*Home Guard 1942. (Rotherham Advertiser)*

In August 1942, a lone German plane dived out of the clouds (some people saw the Nazi markings clearly) after noticing tents at the Middle Lane side of the park. Four bombs were dropped; 'Holidays at Home' were in full swing, it is thought that it may have been mistaken for a military camp. One of the bombs landed just inside the Middle Lane entrance and the crater mark can be seen during very dry spells in the summertime, another caused a crater in the hockey pitch in the grounds of the Girls High School

(Clifton Comprehensive School) and damaged houses on Danum Drive. Luckily, there were no casualties.

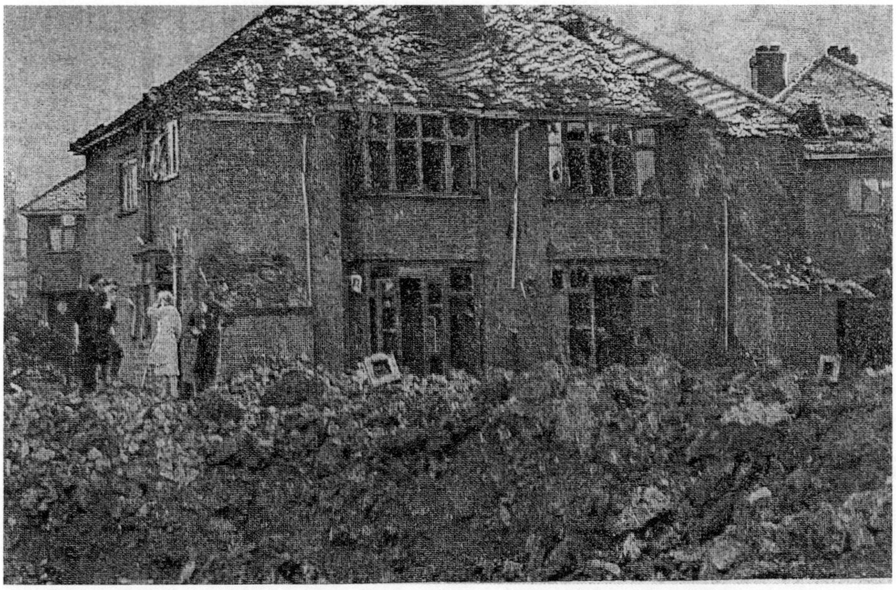

*Bomb damaged properties in Danum Drive, August 1942. (Janet Crowther)*

Contributions by the people of Rotherham for the war effort helped fund a spitfire fighter aircraft and a warship. The spitfire played a role in defending the British fleet at Scapa Flow and the warship HMS Rotherham took the surrender of the Japanese Navy in Singapore in 1945.

A barrage balloon, manned by the WAAF's, hovered in the sky near the sunken garden.

During the Sheffield blitz, incendiary bombs fell onto the Bowling Green; fortunately, the prompt action of the Fire Wardens saw all flames extinguished before the bombers flew over. The bowling green keepers at this time were Mr Hudson and Joe Uttley.

Torrential rail did not dampen spirits in V.J. Day in 1945. A thanksgiving service was held around the bandstand and afterwards, a band played 'up to a late hour there was "free for all dancing".

The park's emergency water tanks were dismantled in May 1945.

Just after this time in 1946, the first bananas arrived in Rotherham.

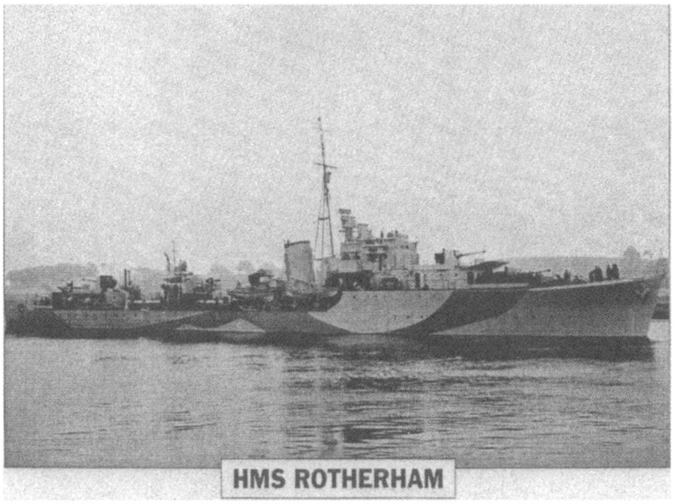

## 26 HOLIDAYS AT HOME 1942 – 1956

The very popular 'Holidays at Home' ran through the school summer holidays during the war years and up until 1956.

The arena area, provided a packed entertainment programme for all the park goers, it included high wire acts, concerts and sports. Motorbike racing was always the finale and the trophies awarded to the race winners can still be seen in Clifton Park Museum.

Holidays at home, Clifton Park 1939=1945

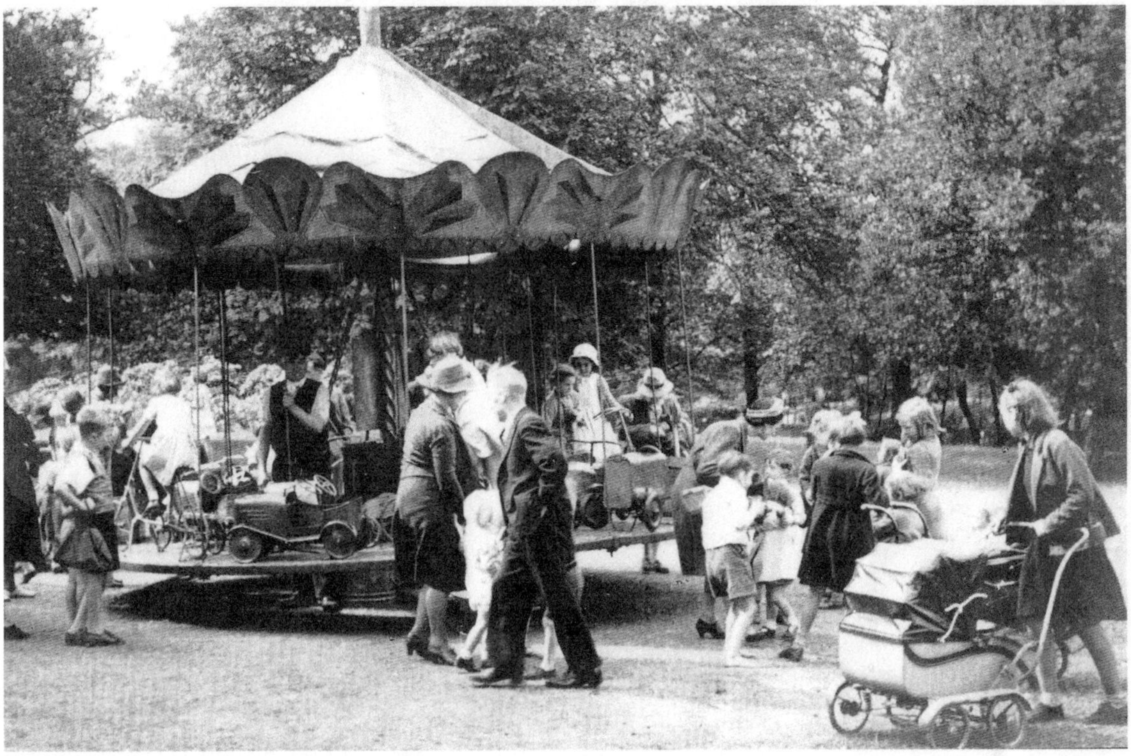

*Holidays at home. (Rotherham Archives)*

In 1942, fifty tons of sand brought from Filey beach enabled the children to make sandcastles adding to the attractions of the Paddling Pool. Beach huts and Pierrot Shows were provided for the grown-ups.

When the Events Programme was produced in 1943, due to paper control not more than 180 square inches of paper per issue was allowed; only 7,000 could be printed and sold for 1d each without a loss, if they were sold for 2d a good profit could be made.

The 1944 programme included a production of "The Gondoliers", boxing from "The Boys Club", 6-a-side football, bowls competitions, sheep dog demonstrations and military bands. Children's events included a sandpit, ten donkeys, "Aunty Rene" and Punch and Judy.

Canal barge trips were organised for July 1944; unfortunately, the Ministry of Supply would not allow Waddington's to take a barge away from the essential work of conveying coal and the arrangements were cancelled.

The Alfresco Theatre was situated facing into the park near the Doncaster Road entrance. A platform was borrowed from Spurley Hey Central School and 1,000 deckchairs provided. One of the star attractions was the well known performer Ronnie Dukes, he was the only boy dancer in Kathy Wright's dancing school.

Evening dances took place at the Bandstand.

A precision motorcycle trick riding team, Mercury Riders, performed in 1951.

The iron railings around the arena were purchased from Rotherham United Football Club in 1953. The public stood around the railings or paid to sit inside them in comfort.

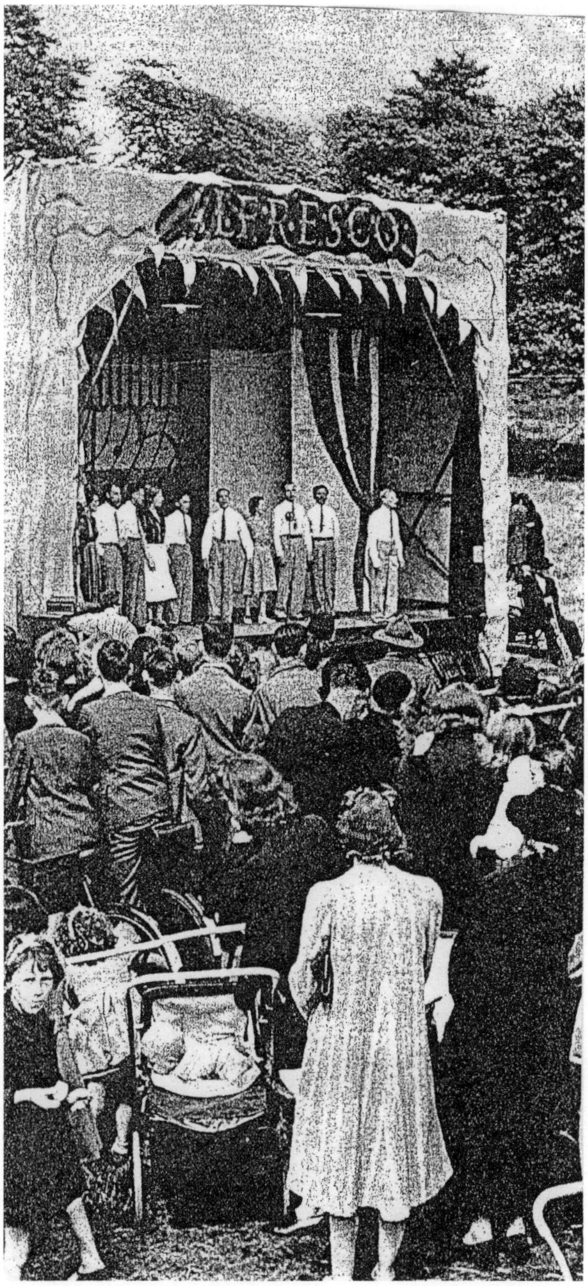

*Civil defence workers at Rotherham's Casualty Clearing Stations put on a free show for grown-ups. So popular that there is 'standing room only', 29th August 1942*

## Extracts for 'Holidays At Home - 1942'

His Worship The Mayor: Councillor A.E. BARLOW
The Town Clerk: Chas. L. DES FORGES, C.B.E.
Chairman of Holidays at Home Committee: Councillor G.A.BARKER
Vice-Chairman: Councillor W. HEWITT

**FOREWORD**

Local Authorities throughout the Country were asked by the Government to provide programmes of attraction during the usual Holiday period of the year.

Those who take advantage of this scheme will be truly wise. By staying at home, they will ease the already overburdened travelling facilities; they will save themselves the anxiety of searching for accomodation; they will spend less and, by investing the savings wisely, will help the War effort. They will be able to enjoy themselves to the full, for there are events to entertain them in Rotherham on every day during the whole of the four weeks of elementary school holidays.

Clifton park will be the centre of attractions. Please remember that it is one of the finest assets of out town. Respect the trees and shrubs and flowers, for they are your property to enjoy - not to destroy.

Have a happy time during these thirty days, and you will go back to your work - whether it be in the Forces, or in works or shops or offices - refreshed both in mind and body, and better able to play your part in bringing the war to a speedy and successful ending.

Mayor Barlow
Chairman Barker
GENERAL INFORMATION
"Holidays At Home"
CLIFTON PARK OFFICE
Birdcage Lodge, Doncaster Road
will be open each day from 1.30pm to deal with general enquiries
Telephone: Rotherham 16

Refreshments: A Marquee near the Formal Gardens in Clifton Park will be open each day to serve light refreshments so far as the wartime food situation permits.

A Creche (opposite the Paddling Pool, Clifton Park) will be open each day to care for children between the ages of 2 and 5 (inclusive) for limited periods.

Lost Children should be taken to THE CRECHE where they will be looked after until claimed.

Lost property should be taken to the CLIFTON PARK OFFICE, Birdcage Lodge, or to the POLICE STATION.

First-Aid Tents, staffed by members of the St. John Ambulance Brigade and Nursing Division will be situated near the COTTENHAM ROAD ENTRANCE to Clifton Park and will be open EVERY DAY.

Deck Chairs will be available in Clifton Park for members of the public at a charge of 6d. per day. 3d. will be refunded on return of the chair in good condition.

Seaside Tents: A limited number of seaside tents will be available in Clifton Park at a charge of 1/6 per day (including 2 deckchairs).

All Programmes are sublect to CANCELLATION or ALTERATION WITHOUT NOTICE. Latest details regarding Programmes will be published every Saturday in the Local Press.

SPECIALLY FOR CHILDREN

Seaside Donkeys will be near the Bandstand in Clifton Park, each morning, afternoon and evening (except Sundays). Some of them will visit Greasbrough Recreation Ground during the afternoons of 27th July, 6th., 14th and 19th. August. Others may visit other parts of the Borough, at times to be arranged.

The PADDLING POOL, Clifton Park, will be open - make good use of it.

A Sand Pit will be made in Clifton Park opposite the Paddling Pool. Please keep it clean.

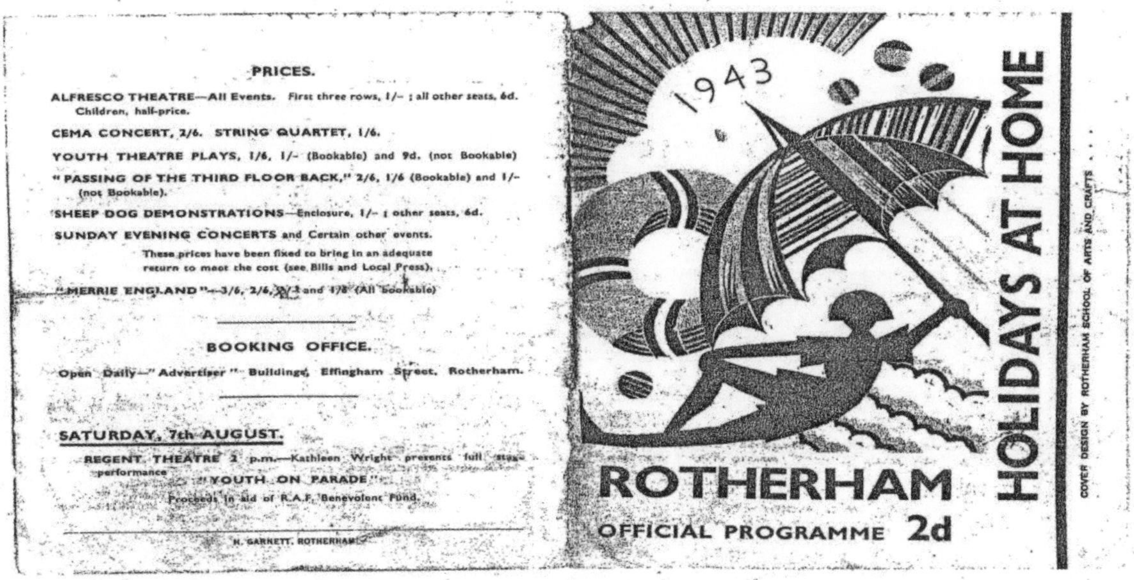

PRICES.

ALFRESCO THEATRE—All Events. First three rows, 1/- ; all other seats, 6d. Children, half-price.

CEMA CONCERT, 2/6. STRING QUARTET, 1/6.

YOUTH THEATRE PLAYS, 1/6, 1/- (Bookable) and 9d. (not Bookable)

"PASSING OF THE THIRD FLOOR BACK," 2/6, 1/6 (Bookable) and 1/- (not Bookable).

SHEEP DOG DEMONSTRATIONS—Enclosure, 1/- ; other seats, 6d.

SUNDAY EVENING CONCERTS and Certain other events.

These prices have been fixed to bring in an adequate return to meet the cost (see Bills and Local Press).

"MERRIE ENGLAND"—3/6, 2/6, [illegible] and 1/8 (All bookable)

BOOKING OFFICE.

Open Daily—"Advertiser" Buildings, Effingham Street, Rotherham.

SATURDAY, 7th AUGUST.

REGENT THEATRE 2 p.m.—Kathleen Wright presents full stage performance "YOUTH ON PARADE"

Proceeds in aid of R.A.F. Benevolent Fund.

H. GARNETT, ROTHERHAM



(Rotherham Archives)

## 27 SUNSHINE CORNER

*'Sunshine Corner it's so jolly fine,*
*It's for children up to ninety-nine,*
*All are welcome,*
*Seats are given free,*
*Clifton Sunshine Corner is the place for me!'*

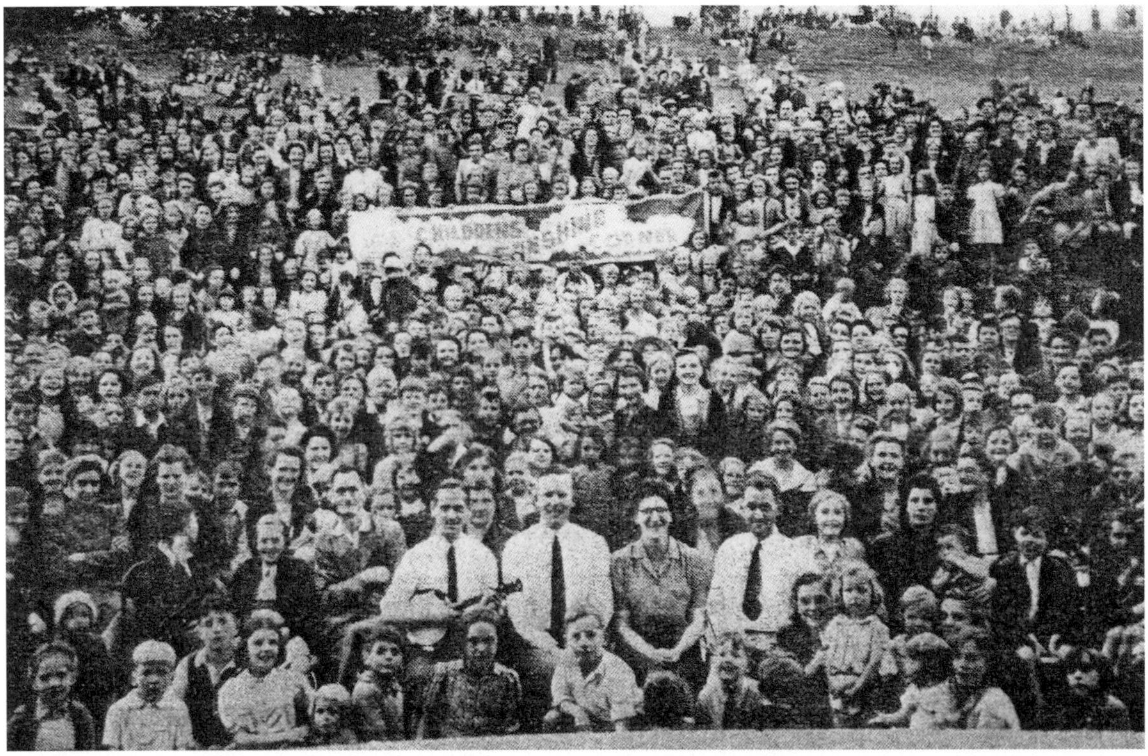

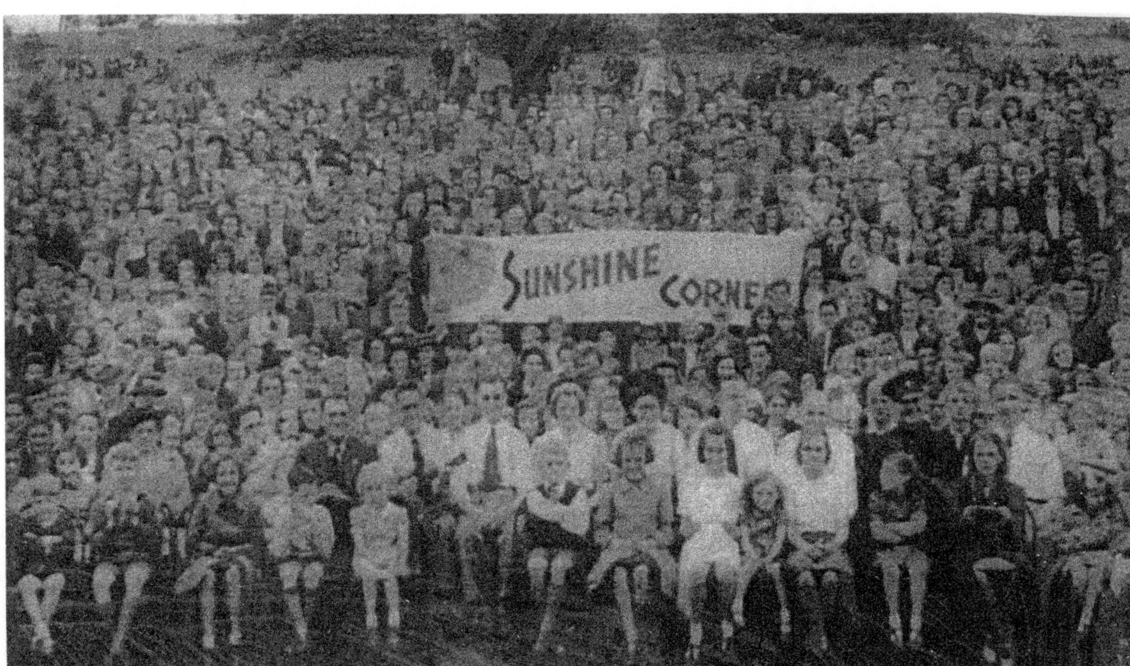


*Sunshine corner, 1940's to 1950's. (Rotherham Archives)*

Many, many children and adults sang the Sunshine Corner signature tune with great gusto around the bandstand between 1942 and 1952. Today, those children are grandparents who still sing the song to grandchildren and their friends when they speak about their childhood. The signature tune for the TV programme, Only When I Laugh, was filched from Sunshine Corner.

*"I am h-a-p-p-y, I am h-a-p-p-y,*
*I know I am, I'm sure I am,*
*I am h-a-p-p-y."*

Restrictions imposed during the war years affected travelling and the blackout and rationing did not help matters. The Local Authority set up an entertainment programme called 'Holidays at Home'.

Archie Biddle, an Elim Minister, asked for permission to use Clifton Park bandstand, with PA equipment, piano and other instruments plus seating for the Elim Christian Centre and their members. Church members assisted 'Uncle Archie', including 'Auntie Madge' an excellent pianist, a drummer, 'Uncle Reg' Moffatt a violinist plus another sister and four men. Everyone was called 'cousins'.

One August bank holiday the attendance topped 3,000 people.
All the songs sung had actions and the choruses were painted on large linen sheets. Singing competitions were held for the children and the adults, sweets were given as prizes to the person who got the loudest clap!

Sunshine Corner always ended with a prayer:

*'Thank you for the world so sweet,*
*Thank you for the food we eat,*
*Thank you for the birds that sing,*
*Thank you God for everything.'*

'Uncle Archie' retired to Paignton in Devon. In 2004, Sunshine Corner was 'revisited' around the bandstand and Uncle Archie Biddle sent everyone his best wishes from his retirement home.

2012 he reached the grand age of 97, still bright and cheery. He died in Torquay, October 2013.

Sunshine Corner stood for decency and emphasised the moral duty of children to obey their parents, teachers and to respect their elders. They were encouraged to attend church or Sunday School.

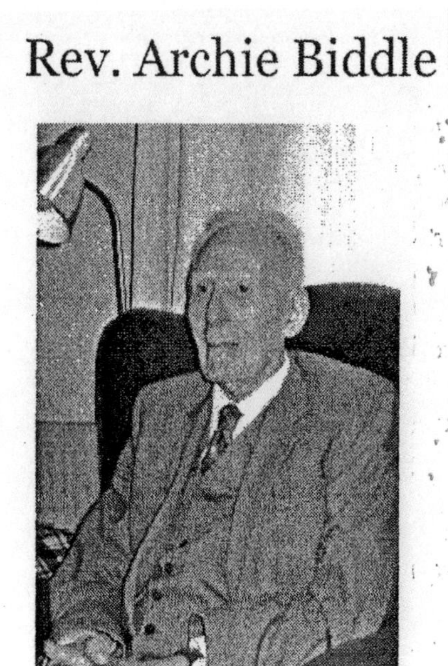


*'Uncle Archie'. (Anon)*

## 28 SPORT AND RECREATION

Old council notices indicate that recreational facilities were established features in the estate between the 1883 sale and the purchase by Rotherham Corporation in 1891.

In October 1885, Clifton Park Football Club played their first match.

There was a Clifton Lawn Tennis Club and references are made to a cricket ground near to Parkfield Road.

The four hard tennis courts, planned in 1914 were finally laid out in1923 on the site of the kitchen garden to the south side of the house. These are still well used throughout the year to this day.

In 1924, bowling greens were created near the tennis courts.

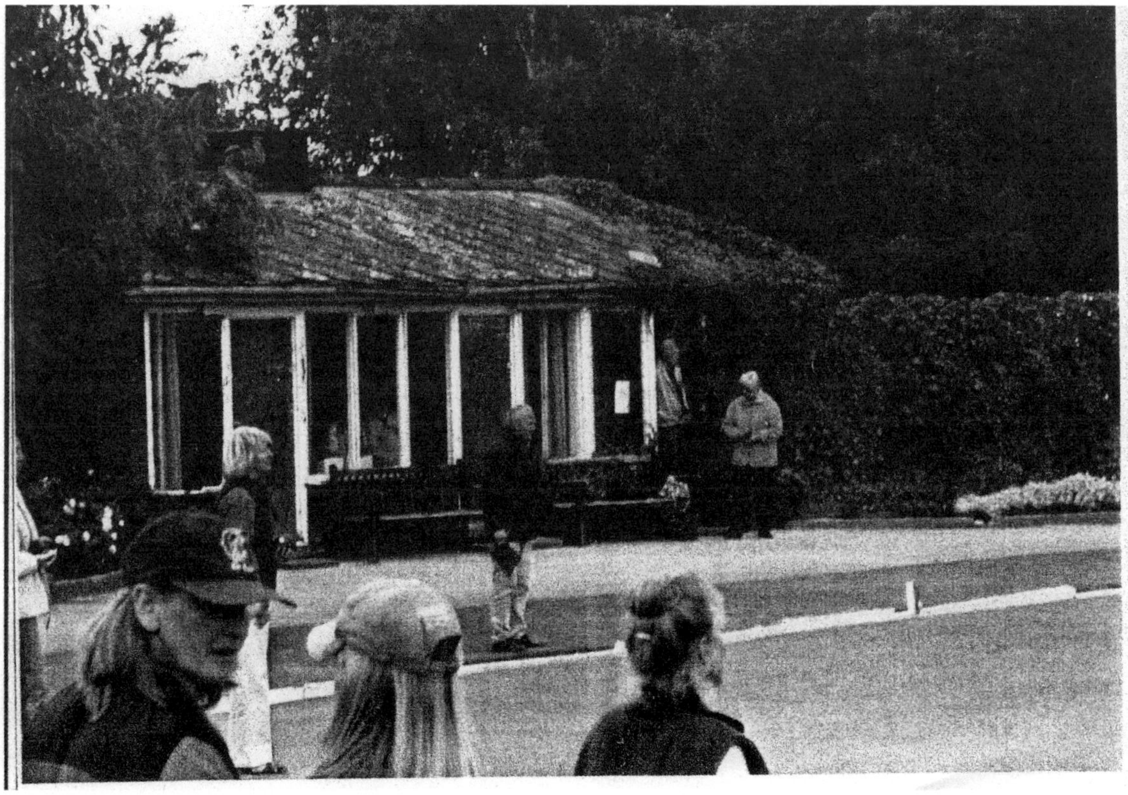

*Reading room 1999. (Author's photograph)*

October 1936, number one bowling green was awarded the highest number of points that has ever been awarded under the National Bowling Green competition, held nationwide. It now has four bowling greens, the fourth was opened on 27th July 1948. It is one of the few places or parks that has this number of greens, enabling it to host large tournaments.

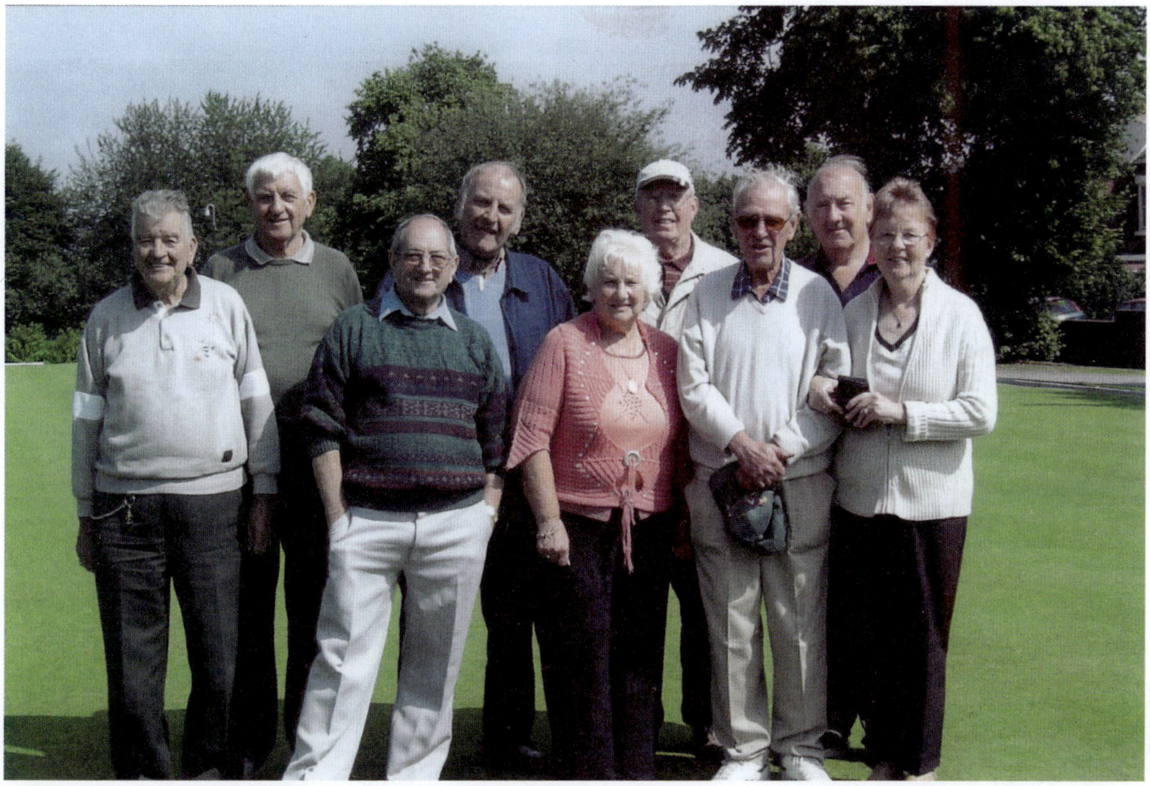

*Clifton Park bowling club, circa 2005. (Author's photograph)*

A shelter was built (with a radiator) by the bowling green in 1935 and a club for older gentlemen was formed there on the 10th September 1938. Twenty men joined the club with an estimated total age of 1,600 years! it being extremely popular with industrial veterans of the County Borough. Gifts, including pictures, seats and clocks were given. The members proudly painted and decorated it. This was known as the reading room or the 'old men's hut', sadly it burnt down and had to be demolished in October 2002.

A bowling pavilion was built in 1974 and named the Duffield Bowling Pavilion after Alderman C. Duffield, but was sadly destroyed by fire in September 1996.

Cycling was allowed between the hours of 6 am to 9 am when the park was first opened, by 1926 the hours were reduced to 6am to 8am !

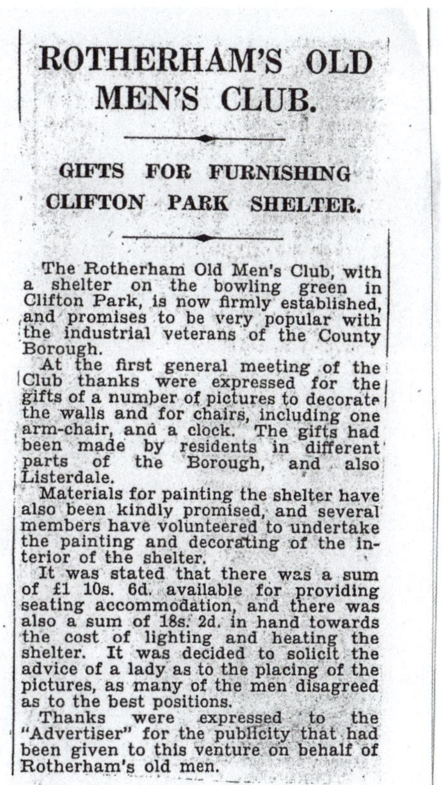

**ROTHERHAM'S OLD MEN'S CLUB.**

**GIFTS FOR FURNISHING CLIFTON PARK SHELTER.**

The Rotherham Old Men's Club, with a shelter on the bowling green in Clifton Park, is now firmly established, and promises to be very popular with the industrial veterans of the County Borough.

At the first general meeting of the Club thanks were expressed for the gifts of a number of pictures to decorate the walls and for chairs, including one arm-chair, and a clock. The gifts had been made by residents in different parts of the Borough, and also Listerdale.

Materials for painting the shelter have also been kindly promised, and several members have volunteered to undertake the painting and decorating of the interior of the shelter.

It was stated that there was a sum of £1 10s. 6d. available for providing seating accommodation, and there was also a sum of 18s. 2d. in hand towards the cost of lighting and heating the shelter. It was decided to solicit the advice of a lady as to the placing of the pictures, as many of the men disagreed as to the best positions.

Thanks were expressed to the "Advertiser" for the publicity that had been given to this venture on behalf of Rotherham's old men.

*Rotherham old men's club, October 1938*

## PARKS AND CEMETERIES COMMITTEE, 20TH MAY 1903

## CLIFTON PARK BOWLING GREEN AND LAWN TENNIS COURTS
## RULES AND REGULATIONS

1.The Bowling Green and Lawn Tennis Courts shall be open every day except Sunday, from 10 o' clock in the forenoon up to the time the park is closed

2. The charges for the use of the greens and courts shall be as follows:-
(1) for each person using the Bowling Green the sum of 1d. per half-hour.
(2) for each person using the Lawn Tennis Courts 2d for each complete set of games played.

3. Season tickets will be issued at a charge of 7s 6d., and they can be had upon application to the Borough Accountant, Town Hall. Such tickets are not transferable.

4. Players who are not season ticket holders are required to obtain tickets, and all ticket holders must keep in their possession their tickets during the time they are playing in order that they may be able to show them to any authorised servant of the Corporation. Any person not being able to show the ticket will be charged double fee under Rule 2 by the checker. Any player other than a season ticket holder leaving the ground will be required to purchase another ticket before playing again.

5. The order of play shall be as follows:-

Each intending player of party of players shall in order of coming on to the ground and when desirous of playing, place his, or their name or names on a slate provided for the purpose.

On the bowling green no person shall retain the ground for more than half an hour if any other person is waiting to play.

6. No person shall be allowed on the greens or courts except the players engaged in the games.

7.On the bowling green the jack to be placed not less than two yards from the edge of the green or mark.

8. The Curator shall have the power to prohibit play on the greens or courts when he thinks it necessary either on account of the weather or on account of portions of the greens or courts being reserved for the purpose of the herbage, or from any other cause.

9. No person shall be allowed on the Lawn Tennis Courts unless wearing tennis or rubber shoes so as to protect the courts.

10. No stick, umbrella, or other article likely to injure the herbage will be allowed on the greens or courts.

11. No person will be allowed to play on the Bowling Greens without using a mat.

12. No dogs shall be allowed on the ground under any circumstances.

13. Lawn Tennis Clubs may reserve the courts for their own special arrangement with the Parks Committee of the County Borough Council.

14. All persons must leave the greens and courts when the bell rings for closing the park.

15. In all cases of dispute the decision of the Curator of the Park or the person having charge of the greens and courts to be final.

16. No persons shall throw matches or expectorate upon the greens or and courts.

17. Any persons infringing any of the above rules or injuring the bowls or the greens or lawn tennis courts or nets, etc., or using profane or indecent language shall be liable to be ejected from the greens and courts.

By Order, H. HAMPTON COPNALL, Town Clerk.

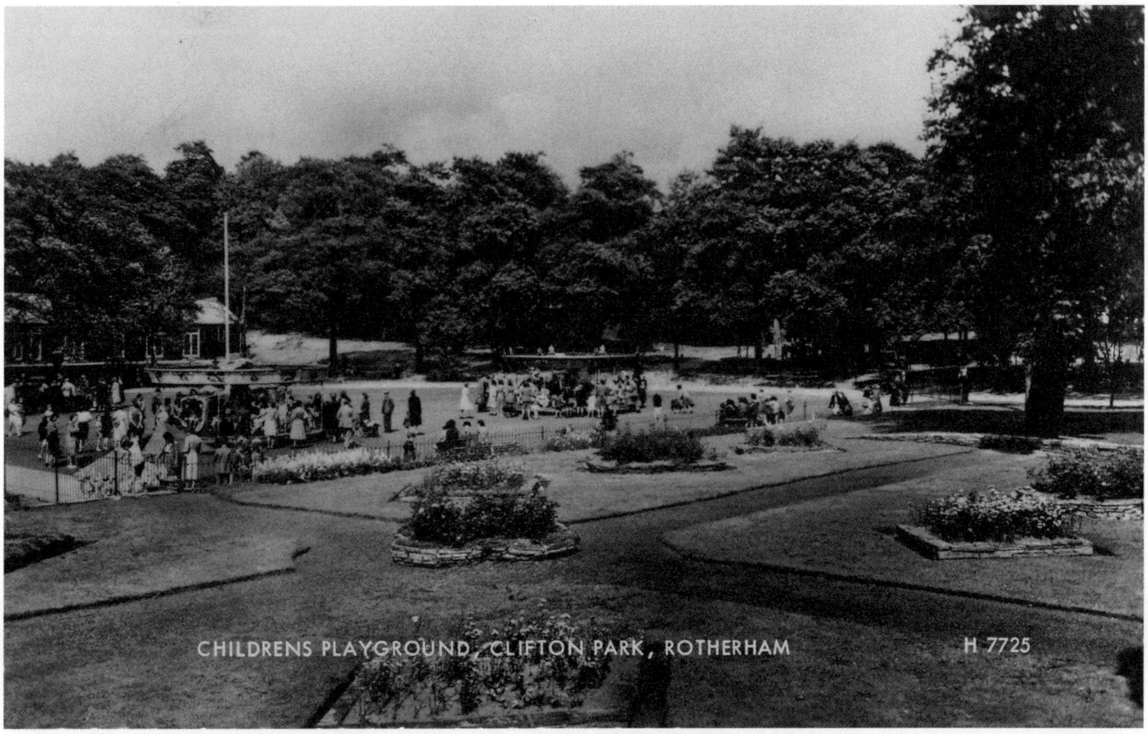


*Children's playground and restful garden in the foreground. (Author's postcard)*

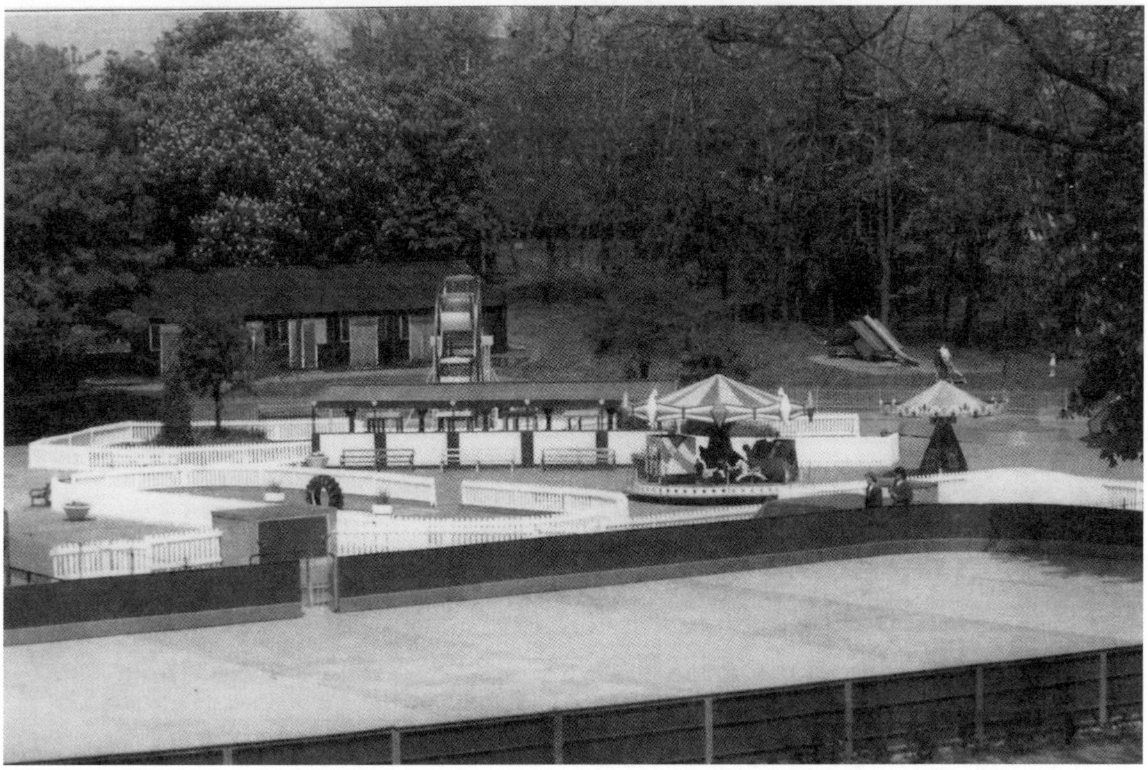

*1984. Roller skating rink dismantled in 2009 for further development. (Rotherham Archives)*

The putting green was opened in 1948 near to the tennis courts but in the 1990's, a car park replaced it.

Clifton Park has a 'town park' character, five minutes from Rotherham town centre, listed in the English Heritage register of parks and gardens; it is used by people for many purposes, sport and games, some to read and eat their lunch, others to use the Museum facilities. Many for the events that are regularly held, and children use it to just thoroughly enjoy themselves. It must not be forgotten, many people walk through on a daily basis to get to and from their place of work, town, and school and exercise their dogs.

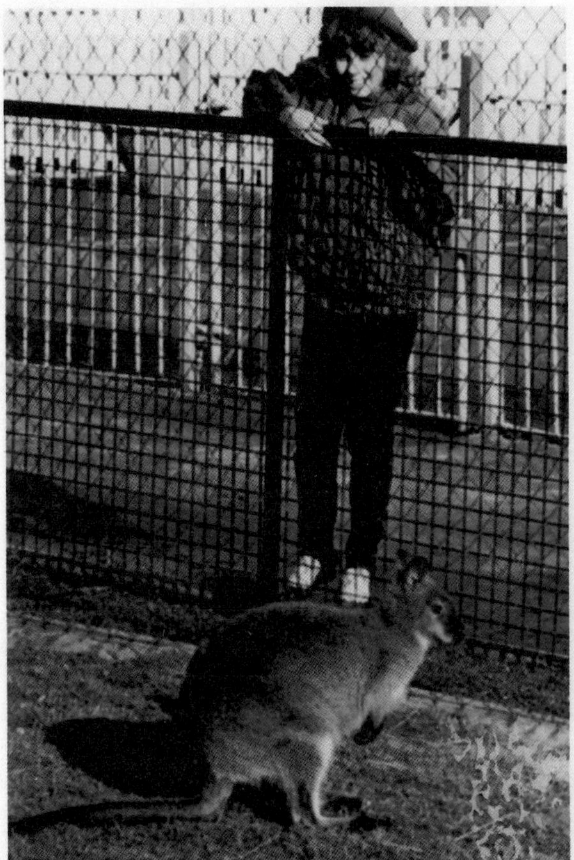

*The Wallaby and Laurie Harrison at the aviary in Clifton Park. (Pamela Harrison)*

Post war development and recreational facilities have improved over the years and moved with the times. The original aviaries and peacock houses were demolished in February 1930. 1974 saw the introduction of a pet's corner and aviary, geese, peacocks, rabbits, goats, hens, chicks, canaries, parakeets and a wallaby lived there. Many park goers enjoyed it until its closure in the 1990's.

May 1984, a roller skating rink opened near the paddling pool until further development took place in 2009.

An eleven hole crazy golf course was built near to the bowling greens in 1985. It was built on the site of the old greenhouses and very successful until its closure in 2009.

A basketball court was also provided on the site of the old tennis court, although not enclosed it is used daily. 2004 a skateboard and BMX arena was built.

## 29 PADDLING POOL

What can be said about THE paddling pool, from its opening in 1939 until its closure in 2007, is that nearly everyone in Rotherham has dipped a toe or more into it. That is 70 years of happiness.

In October 1937, plans for a children's paddling pool, on the site of the lake were approved with an estimated cost of £3,500. This cost included the drainage and the filtration plant. It was also known as Barker's paddling pool after Alderman G. A. Barker, the chairman of the Parks and Cemeteries Committee at that time.

It measured 100 feet in diameter and had a depth of between 5" and 12", it was enclosed so children could not stray. Seats and a small garden overlooked the pool enabling the parents to rest whilst watching their children. A small glass fronted hut or reading room was at the rear of the pool.

No formal opening of the paddling pool was held in August 1939; it is said the children did an "unofficial opening" themselves with great joy during the Easter holidays, April 1939. The weather at this time being very warm.

The structure remained the same throughout its years and well maintained. Alas in 2007, the pump blew and it was irreparable.

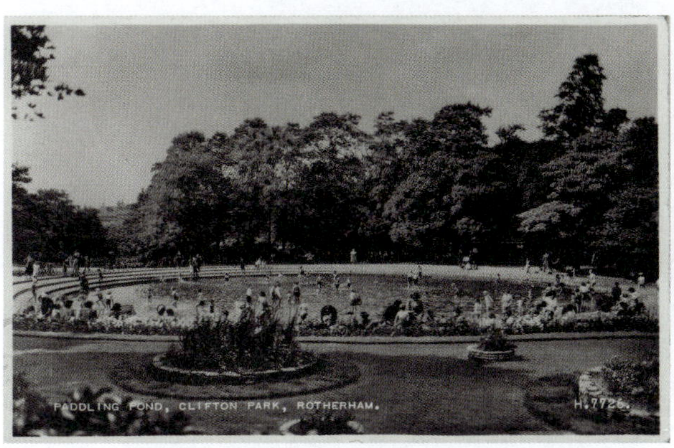


*Paddling pool 1955. (Author's postcard)*

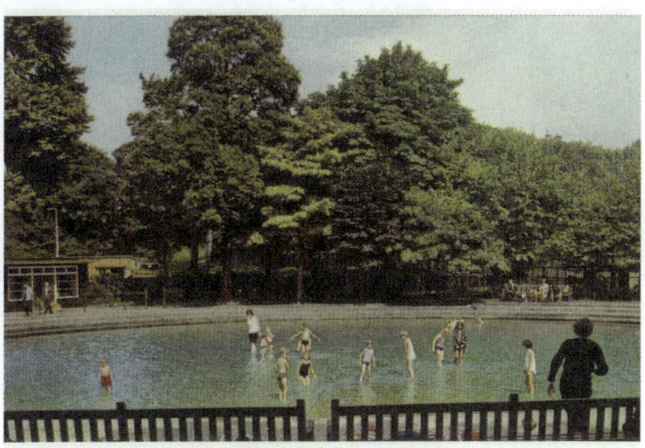

*Paddling pool 170. (Rotherham Archives)*

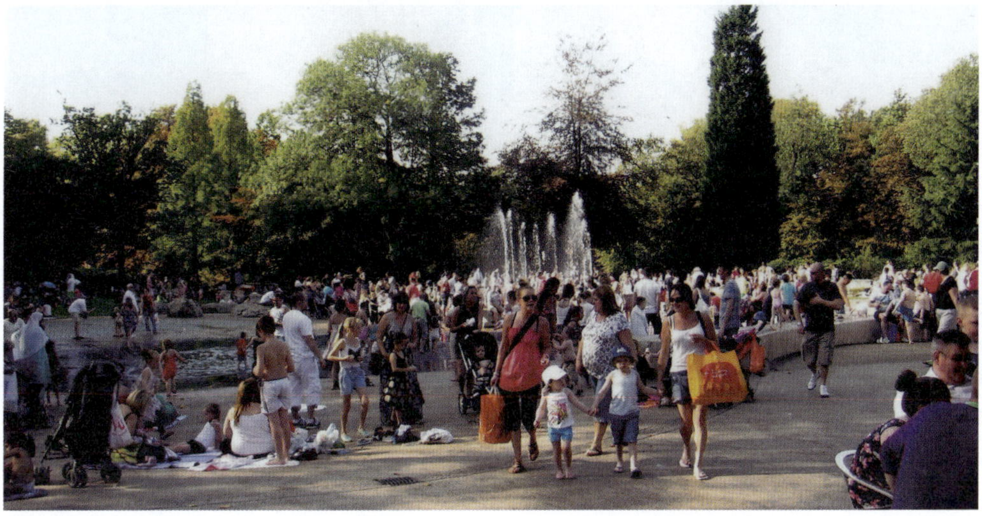

*Hoards of children enjoying the new water play feature, 2011. (Author's photograph)*

## 30 CHILDREN'S ROUNDABOUTS

1939 was an exciting year for children in Clifton Park. The roundabouts opened and a small train went round and round much to everyone's delight. Tickets were bought on a strip entitling the children to ride on Cinderella's coach and horses, a stagecoach or motorcar.

Over the years, these were replaced and updated with new models. In its last year, the helter-skelter became a firm favourite.

To the rear of the roundabouts a café was built, this remained opened all day during the summer months selling teas and ice creams.

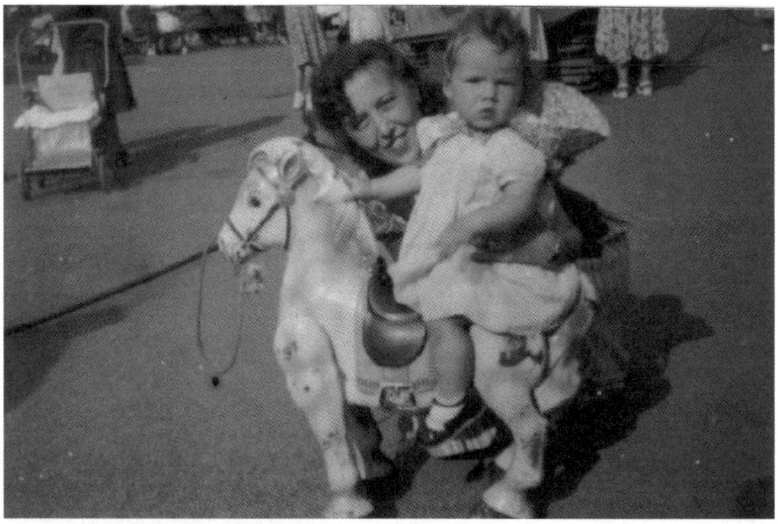

*Mobo horses for small children. (Katrine Greenwood)*

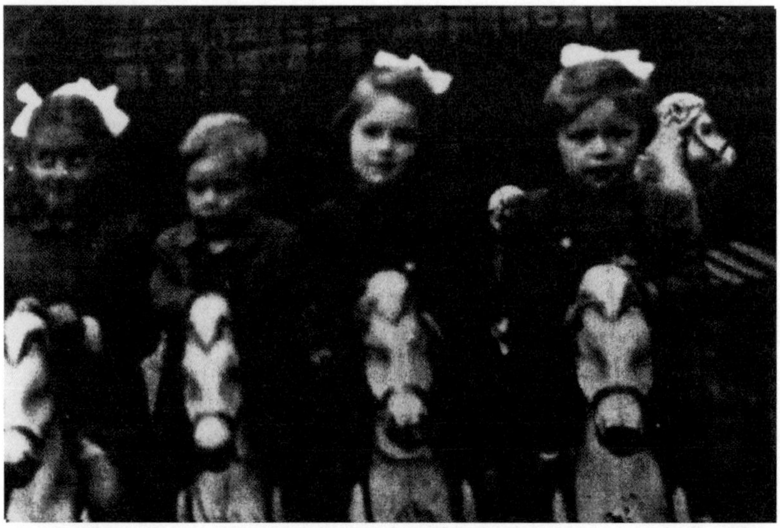

*Four children enjoying the Mobo horses. (Unknown)*

For many years, a track around the perimeter was used for mobo horses for small children and the 'up and down' bikes for older children and adults. Few accidents occurred on these bikes but they gave a lot of fun to the people who attempted to ride on them. The bikes could be seen throughout the country and were often called 'bucking bronco'. The four Hawtin brothers made them in Blackpool. They needed the unusual motion of propelling it forward by means of the 'nether portions' instead of the feet. The rider's weight then transmitted from the saddle through a crank movement to the hub of the rear wheel.

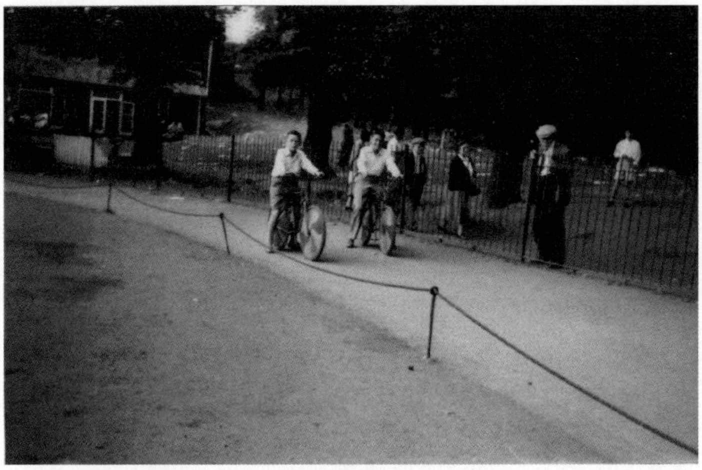

*'Up and down' bikes, 1950's. (Mrs. Mary Chapman)*

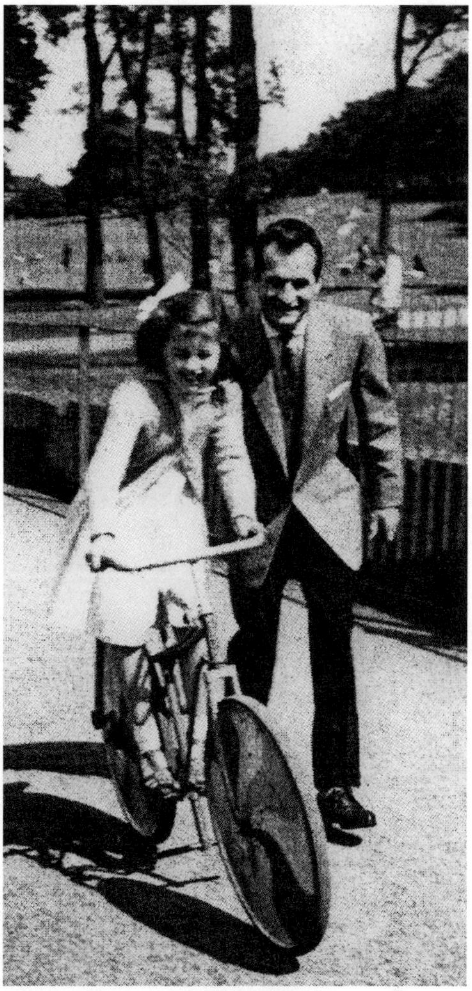

*Hawtin Bike*

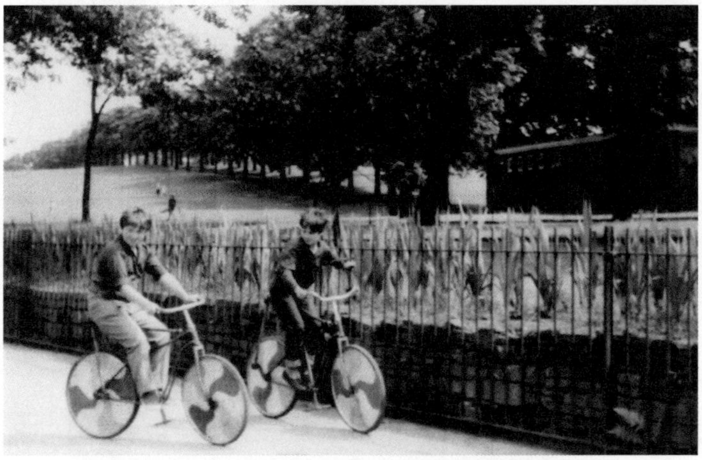

*David and Peter Winter riding the Hawtin bicylces, 1960's (David Winter)*

The roundabouts opened at Whitsuntide until the end of August each year. In 1976, one of the hottest summers on record, 500,000 tickets were sold for the rides, another record-breaking number!

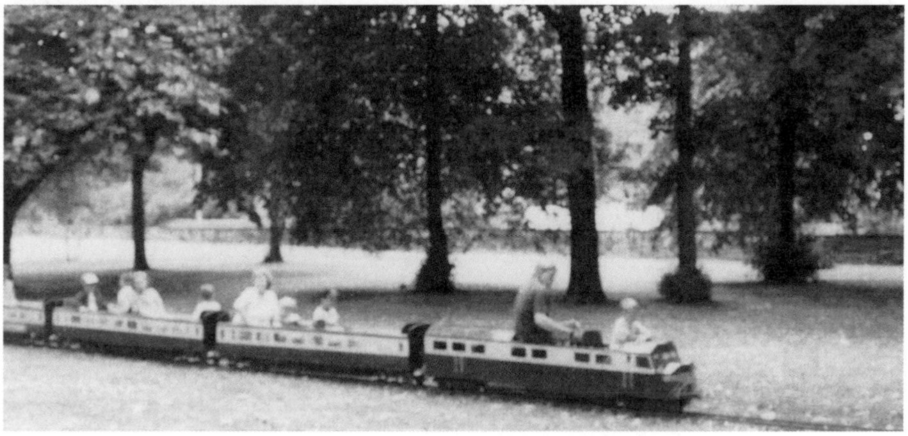

*Miniature train opposite the Memorial garden, 1994. (Rotherham Archives)*

In 1989, Mr Dave Perry built a 100-yard long children's railway on the grass opposite the Memorial Garden. It closed in 1997.

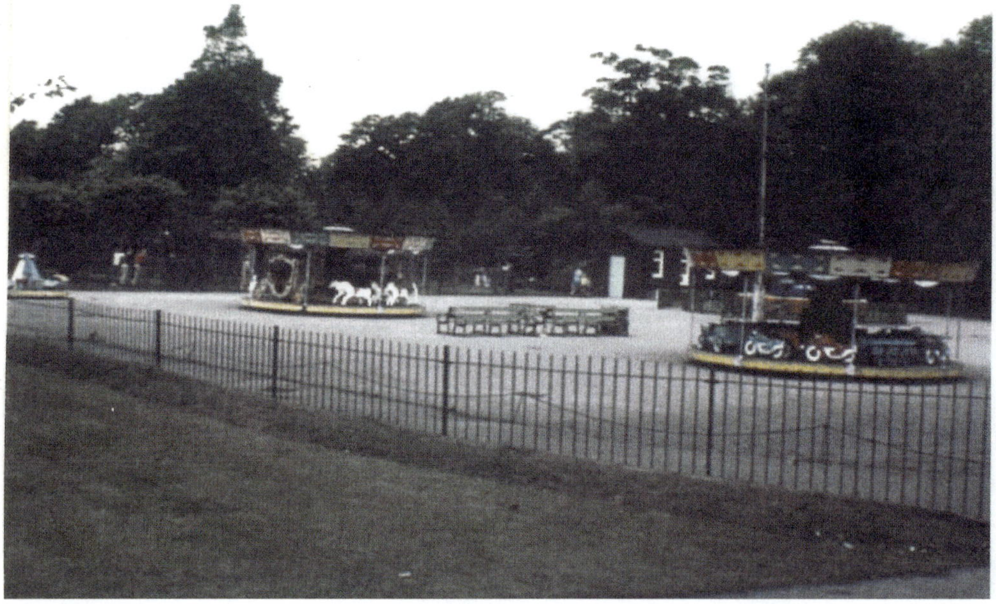

*Clifton Park amusements, 1962. (Rotherham Archives)*

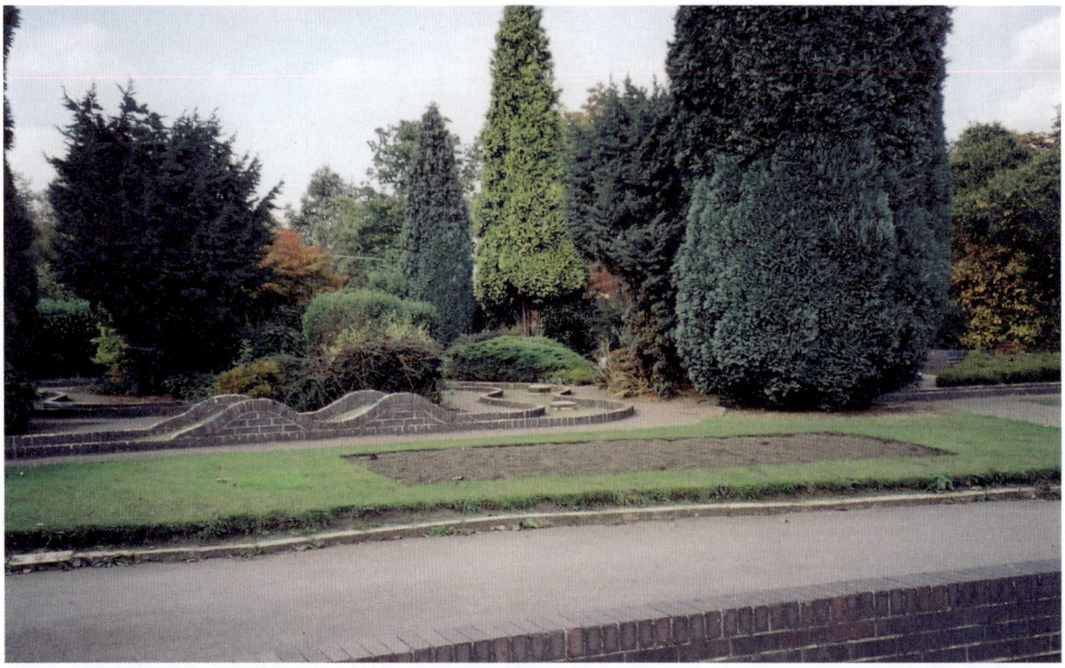

*Crazy Golf near the bowling greens, Autumn 2009. (Author)*

Children's play area, Clifton Park 1991.5

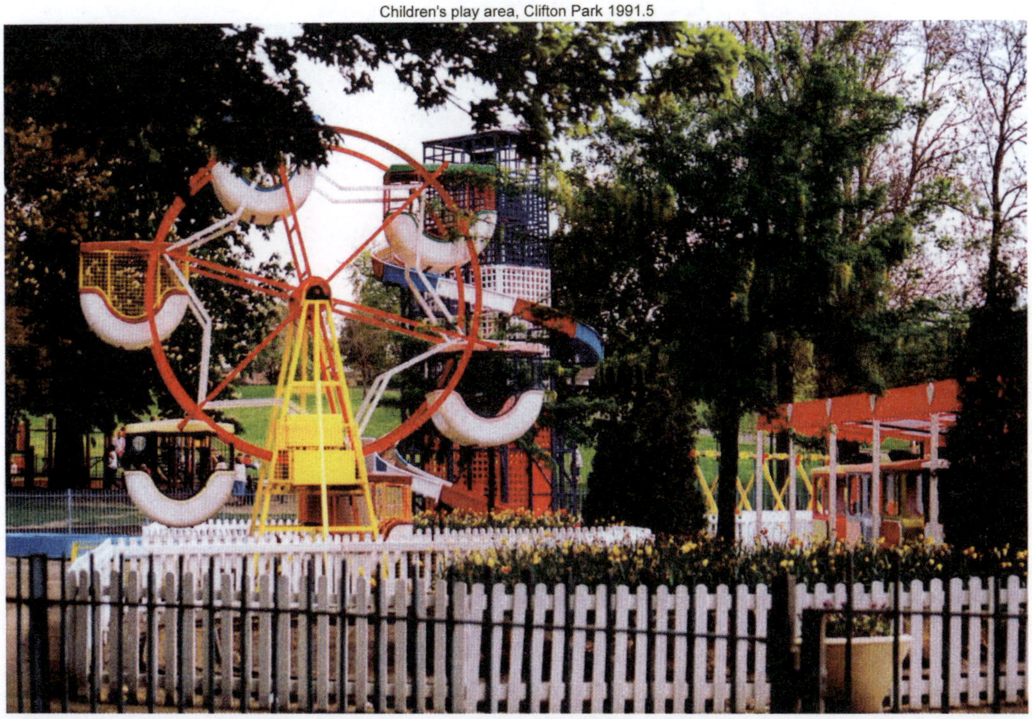

*Children's play area. (Author)*

An 18 hole miniature golf course was added in 2009 and upgraded further in 2010/11. The improvements included, it's size, the use of water and altogether much more interesting and fun.

In 2004, Jay Wheatley took over the running of the roundabouts and installed new rides including bumping cars, a train and a roller coaster. All the rides and slots machines are very different from 1939 but the children are the same, laughing and smiling and enjoying their visit to Clifton Park!

Summer of 2010 saw the introduction of a land train, called 'The Clifton Express'. There are two stops where you can board and alight. Take the train from the stop at the rear of the museum and travel halfway round the park to the amusements. Alternatively, board the train at the amusements and travel the halfway up to the museum.

## 31 CLIFTON PARK DONKEYS

In 1942, ten donkeys were introduced into the park to provide rides for children. The donkey's bells could be heard as they trotted along the roads into Clifton Park from where they were stabled, the big pens to the rear of Herringthorpe Playing Fields pavilion. In 1979/80 they transferred to stabled accommodation in the park and when they were not at 'work', children visited them with carrots and other goods to eat.

The donkey rides were just behind the playground near to the 'camel' tree.

In 1960, the cost of a donkey ride in Clifton Park was 3d.

In 1997, these lovable animals retired.

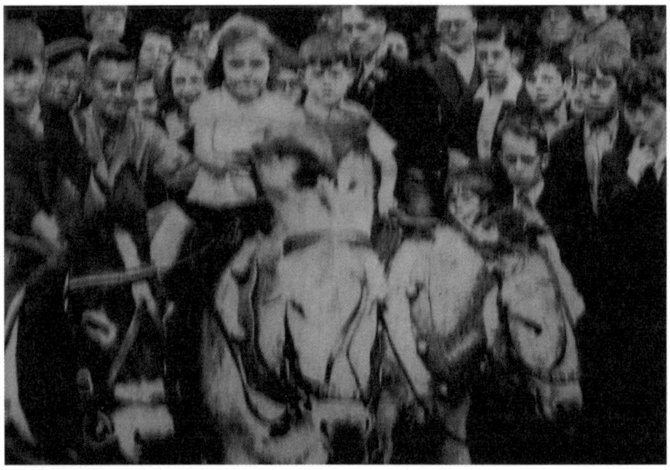

*Donkey rides. (Rotherham Advertiser)*

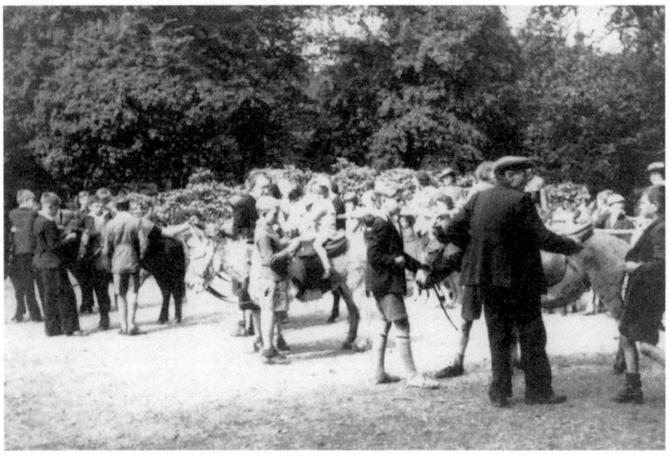

*Clifton Park donkeys, 1937 - 1945. (Rotherham Archives)*

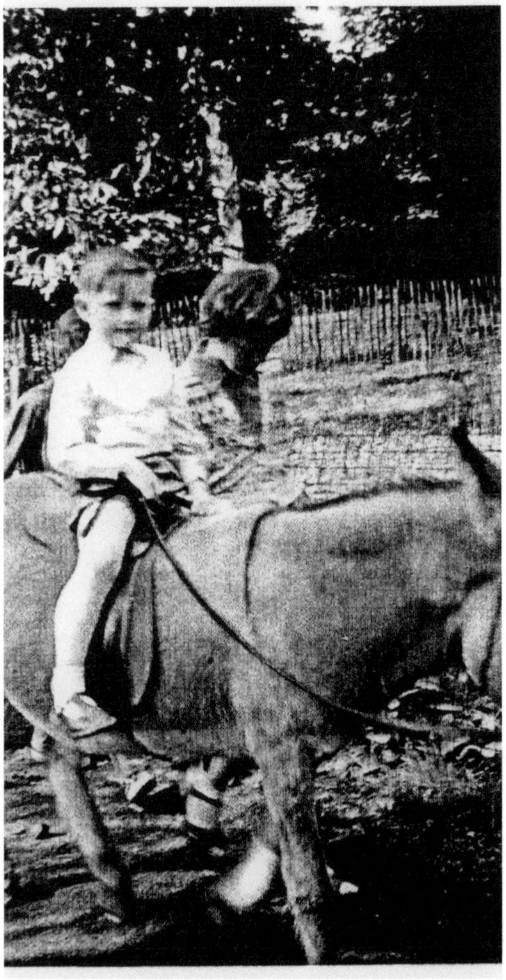

*Mark Wilson 1961 - 1962. (Pauline Wilson)*

## 32 FIREWORK DISPLAYS

The first grand firework display held in Clifton Park was to celebrate its opening on the 25th June 1891.

Since that time, many fireworks and bonfires have been lit to celebrate special events.

On the 12th May 1937, an evening concert of classical music was followed by a spectacular firework display to mark the coronation of King George VI.

Two other memorable firework displays; 1951, Festival of Britain and June 1953 the coronation of Queen Elizabeth II.

In 1969, bonfires were proposed to mark Guy Fawkes Night, but it was not until 1974 that 3,000 people visited Clifton Park for the first municipal bonfire and firework display. This was celebrated annually until its cessation in 1993. Thanks to the Friends of Clifton Park in 2003, it was reintroduced with the added attraction of a funfair provided by William Percival.

An estimated 7,000 people attend the park for this annual display and is enjoyed by people of all ages.

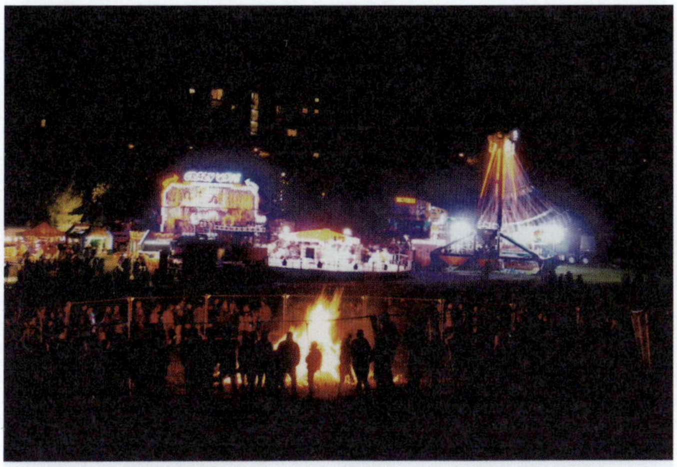

*Bonfire and firework display 2013. (Mr A. Smith Photographer)*

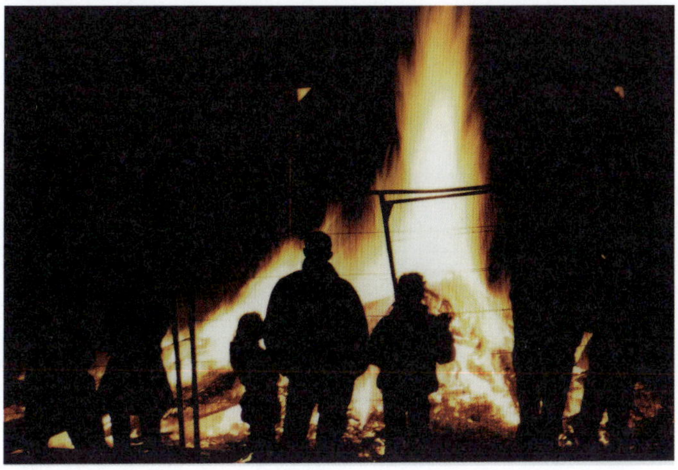

*Friends of Clifton Park bonfire 2013. (Mr A. Smith Photographer)*

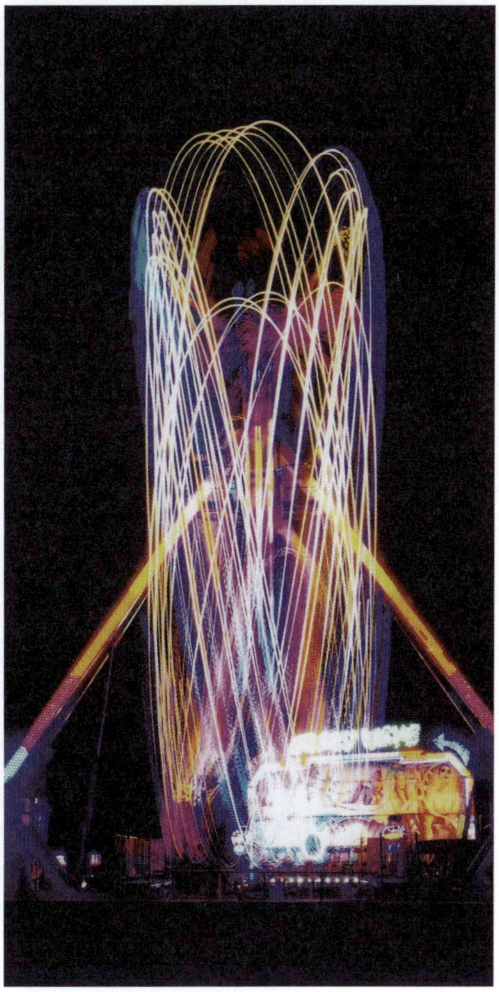

*Bonfire and firework display 2013. (Mr A. Smith Photographer)*

10.0 p.m.—FIREWORKS DISPLAY in Clifton Park, by Messrs. C. T. Brock and Co., Crystal Palace Fireworks Limited.

The Display will commence with a signal aerial maroon and barrage of rockets and magical illumination of the surrounding park. Then will follow showers of confetti from rockets, discharge of shells of fiery jewels, the Jewelled Rainbow, showers of Shimmering Stars, Coral Cascades, Roman Candles, the Jewelled Parasol, festoons of Spring Flowers, etc., etc. Special set pieces will be The Imperial Crown and the letters "G.R." in lines of brilliant fire; a humorous mechanical device, "The Cock Fight;" the Glowing Sunflower;" the Helicopter; a mechanical device, "The Acrobat;" The Star of India; a gigantic shell, 42ins. in circumference, "The Queen Elizabeth;" the Golden Chrysanthemum; the discharge of several special shells containing flashing light-balls and whirls of fire. The display will terminate with a final word-piece "God Save the King," surrounded by a frame of golden fire.

---

NOTE.—His Worship the Mayor (Ald. F. A. Barlow) will attend the Coronation Service in Westminster Abbey, and will, therefore, be unable to be present at the local celebrations.

*Firework display for the coronation of King George VI (Rotherham Advertiser)*

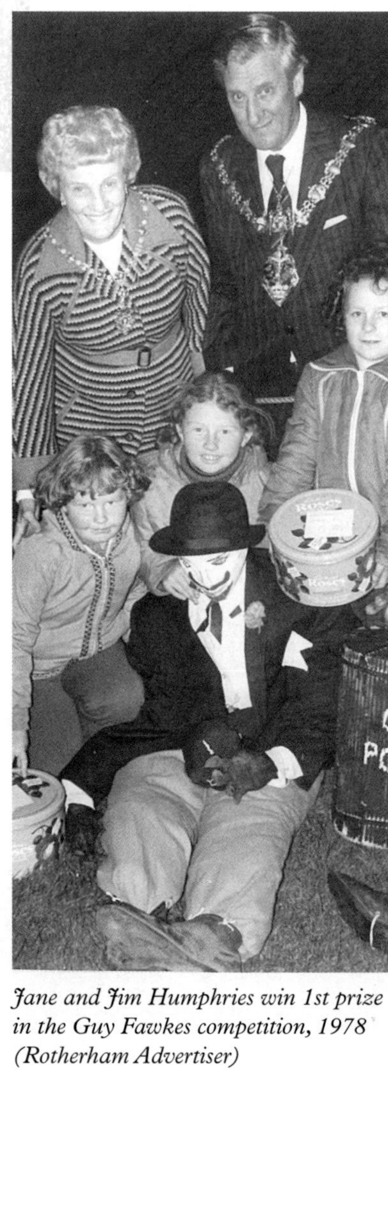

*Jane and Jim Humphries win 1st prize in the Guy Fawkes competition, 1978 (Rotherham Advertiser)*

## 33 EVENTS

Thousands of events have been held in Clifton Park since it opened it gates in 1891 including:

| | |
|---|---|
| 1896 | The first Yorkshire Miners Annual Demonstration was held |
| 1901 | Clifton Park welcomed the Soldiers back from South African War |
| 1909 | Regular gramophone concerts at the bandstand |
| | Annual hospital demonstrations began |
| 1910 | The 5th Battalion York & Lancaster review, over 10,000 spectators watched this review |
| | Railway servant orphans' demonstration |
| 1911 | 22nd June, Coronation festivities for King George V |
| 1917 | Mayor's Belgium Refugees Fund and Local Prisoner of War Fund. |
| 1923 | 28th May The Prince of Wales inspected ex-servicemen and nurses |
| 1931 | 5th July Somme Anniversary Commemoration |
| 1949 | The annual Agricultural and Horticultural shows began |
| 1953 | 11th June Coronation festivities for Queen Elizabeth II |
| | Children's coronation display |
| 1956 | Boy Scouts Association soap box derby |
| 1971 | 28th August Marc Bolan and T. Rex concert |

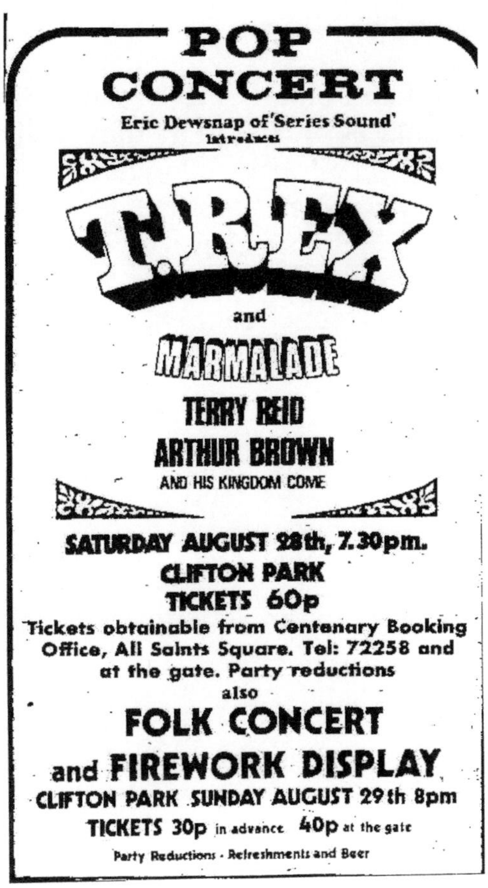


*(Rotherham Advertiser)*

To mark the Coronation of Queen Elizabeth in 1953, a 35-foot flagpole was erected in the arena and 5,000 schoolchildren assembled to sing a Coronation medley, patriotic songs, followed by a demonstration of physical training, and dancing. Around 10,000 people enjoyed the event.

To celebrate the 100 years of Rotherham's Charter in 1971, Clifton Park hosted a circus, band concerts, dog shows, cycle and motor races.

Motoring Weekends were held in June, in 1976 some 20,000 people attended. All the displays and sideshows were enjoyed in the glorious weather of that year.

Many events came year after year to Clifton Park but over time, with the changes in work and leisure patterns of society, people's lives altered as did their needs for entertainment. People will remember with affection the days with the Lambretta Club, the Rotherham Wheeler's Cycling Club, Chipperfield's Circus, the Yorkshire Schools cross-country championships, Wentworth Pony Club, Miners demonstrations,

Lions Club Gala, agricultural shows and Sunday school picnics, Fossetts Circus exhibiting their many animals and Flying Club demonstrations.
Nowadays, many of these events come together in September of each year; over a two-day weekend the Rotherham Show is held, this began in 1979. The Motoring Festival, a vintage car rally and display formerly held on Herringthorpe Playing Fields, was incorporated into the show in 1995. It attracts thousands of people and is one of the largest free shows in the North of England.

A Battle of Britain Memorial flypast honoured Clifton Park at the 1999 Rotherham Show.

A Douglas C47, fondly known as the Dakota, gave a spectacular display during the September 2004 show.

The first Christmas carnival was held in Clifton Park in 2007. Santa Claus visited, the roundabouts were open, bands played, Christmas stalls were busy, and all had a grand time.

We celebrate many different things, often following the USAs lead. In 2009, Clifton Park hosted its first Halloween event and families in fancy dress enjoyed the activities.

Young and old flock into Clifton Park for the large events, but many visit for the rest and peace it gives. On warm, quiet days, families enjoy picnicking or simply walking about.

In January 2010, there was a severe snowfall; families enjoyed playing together throwing snowballs, sledging down the hills, and building snowmen.

The popularity of the park grew due to the ease of travel and more visitors using their own cars. In 1984, a coach park for four vehicles was built as on weekdays during the term time schoolchildren visit. A Sheffield school has brought all their children for their annual school trip, therefore Rotherham should be proud of the facilities they provide. By 1994, it became necessary to upgrade the car parking facilities further.

In the 1980's most urban parks began a spiral of decline when Council Rates were capped. Nationally full time park keepers were removed from their posts allowing standards of maintenance to fall and many parks becoming NO-GO areas.

The 1990's saw the development of Country Parks, with great sums of money invested, gradually the awareness grew that smaller urban parks were suffering from these cutbacks.

Rotherham Council took the decision to construct a different type of play areas for children. Clifton Park had a new Skateboard and BMX area built in 2004 that was well used until newer, upgraded facilities were provided in 2009.

## 34 CLIFTON PARK IN THE 21ST CENTURY

In the 1990's, there was an increase in country parks nationally which was detrimental to many urban parks as less money was available. Play areas, flowerbeds and the infrastructure fell into decay and nationally £64 million pounds was spent fighting vandalism.

Approximately 33 million people use parks each year and the commission for architecture and the built environment argued that antisocial behaviour, vandalism, littering and crime would be reduced if wardens and rangers were introduced. Rotherham did this in 2002.

The Urban Ranger Service, led by Julian Mullins, was introduced as a pilot scheme for the long-term unemployed. It proved successful and became a permanent Ranger Service; Richard Brown still works in the park.

In the same year, the Friends of Clifton Park formed with a lot of support and goodwill from many sources, including Rotherham Metropolitan Borough Councils Culture and Leisure department and it's Director, Phil Rodgers.

The first police bicycle in Rotherham was provided for the Community Police Officer in Clifton Park in 2003 and he could be seen most days, weather permitting, around Clifton Park and district.

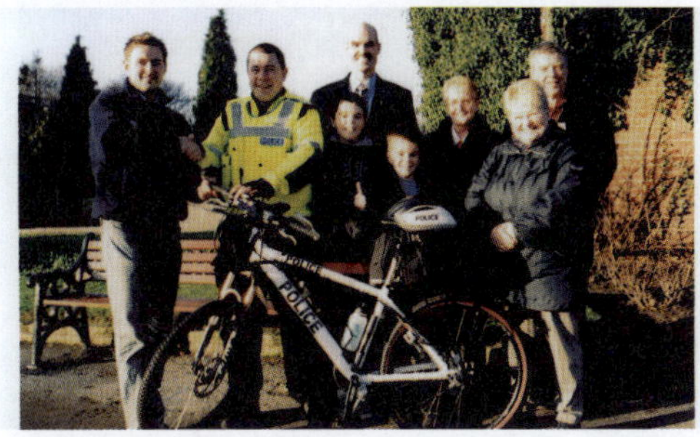

*Friends of Clifton Park and James Cycles presenting a bicycle to PC Ian Spiers for use in the Clifton Park and the community, 2003. (Unkown)*

Work began in 2003 to prepare and submit an application to the Heritage Lottery Fund to renovate Clifton Park. It involved a great deal of planning and hard work by everyone involved. It was a very exciting time. A quote from 'The Garden' in July 2003 said *'a balance has to be struck between what is familiar and treasured by local communities and exciting new design'*.

May 2008, the Heritage Lottery Fund design awarded Rotherham £4.5 million from their 'Parks for People' programme and R.M.B.C.'s contribution was £1.4 million.

Funding at the beginning of 2008 also allowed restoration of the Roman Granary to be carried out, recreation of the Scarp Walk, and a pathway through the glade following an original one, upgrading of the car and coach park and a fence to protect the beech tree.

- Work commenced at the end of September 2008 that included the following areas of the park:
- Construction of the new water play feature, including toilets, changing facilities and kiosk.
- Renovation of the bandstand
- Re-development of the Memorial Garden, including a new water feature.
- Renovation of the Cenotaph
- A garden building with bowling pavilion, multi-function room, Rangers facilities, a courtyard and a community walled garden

- Gates at the main entrance and the Museum entrance
- Boundary fencing
- Renovation of the rock garden
- Planting throughout the park
- Removal of the Grade II listed stone pillars from the Clifton Grove entrance and re-sited at the Museum entrance
- Brick pillars built at Clifton Grove entrance to replace the stone pillars

## MONOLITHS

The Museum already had two information boards giving its history on them and a further six have been added, these can be viewed at the following places:

The memorial rock garden
Cenotaph
The beech tree
Bandstand
Walled garden
Water play
Roman Granary

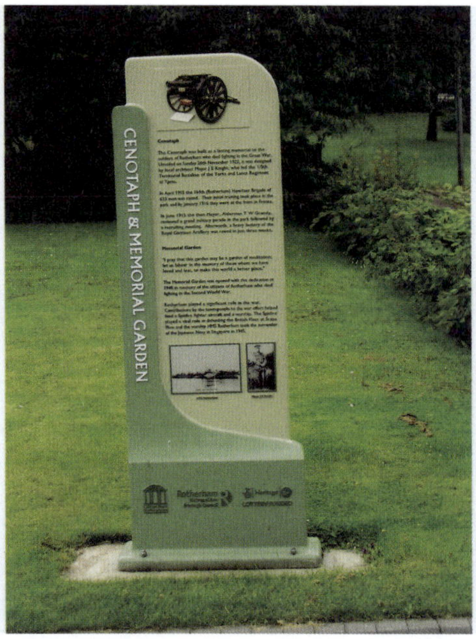


*Monolith in Memorial garden and at the Cenotaph. (Author)*

## TREE CYCLE PROJECT

Working in partnership with South Yorkshire Forest, the timber from the trees felled in the park was used in the buildings and artworks. Demonstrations of tree felling and woodcarving were given in October 2008.

In 2009, due to the extensive ongoing alterations within the park and the second year in its history, Rotherham Show was held in Victoria Park, Rawmarsh.

## THE CENOTAPH

The stone was cleaned and the pathways and steps replaced.

The twelve bronze plaques were restored and the eternal flame on top of the cenotaph re-designed. It was re-dedicated on Remembrance Sunday, 8th November 2009, the Ceremony and Act of Remembrance was led by the Reverend Canon David Bliss, Vicar of Rotherham.

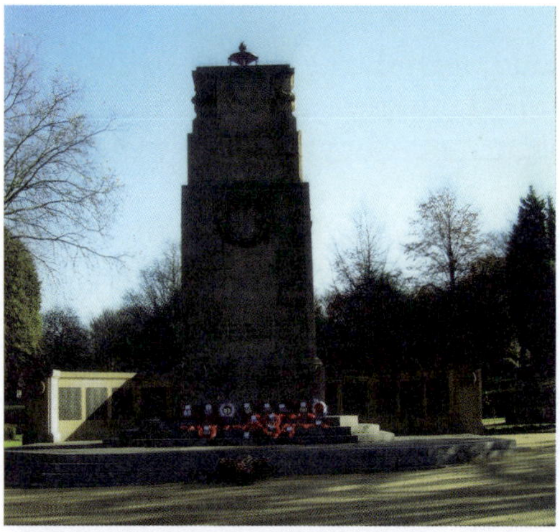

*The Cenotaph following rededication, 8th November 2009. (Author)*

## MAIN GATES AND PILLARS

To the front of the Cenotaph at the main entrance, the stone pillars were restored, beautiful gates designed, and hung; these are very similar to the original ones that were removed for the 'War Effort'.

## MEMORIAL GARDEN

This peaceful garden was re-designed and the stone walls repaired and urns similar to the original placed on the plinths. A more modern water feature has replaced the old fountain. The new flowerbeds planted with box hedging and bedding plants, and it provides a place to sit peacefully and perhaps think of times past.

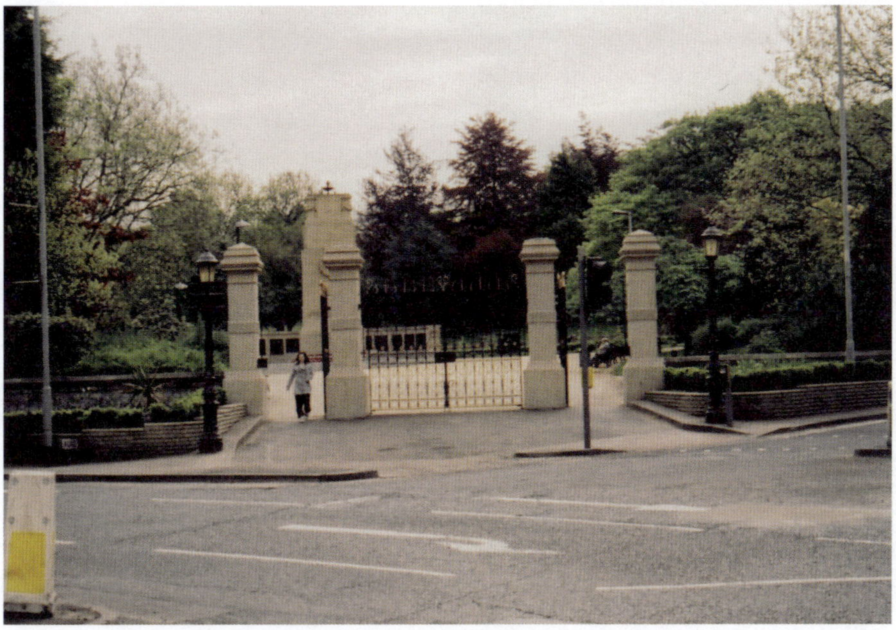

*Gates made to almost identical original design. (Author)*

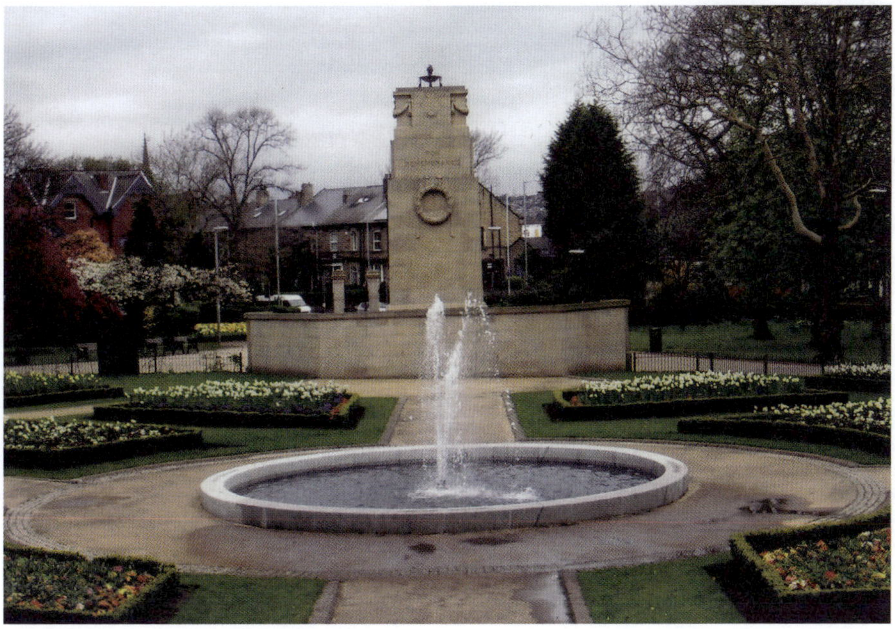

*Memorial garden, Spring 2012. (Author)*

## VICTORIA CROSS FOUNTAIN

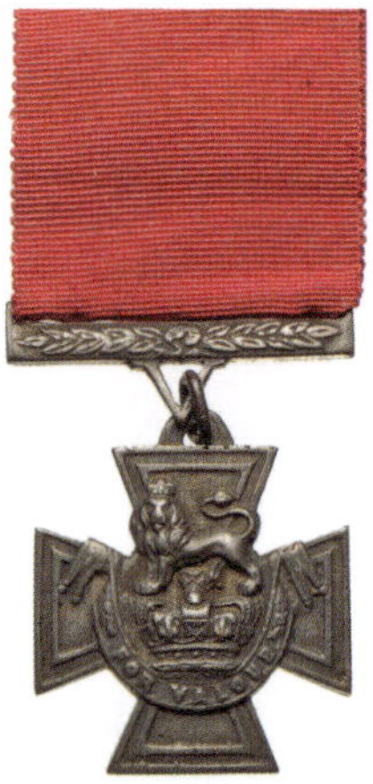

On the 5th October 2011, a dedication service was held to honour Rotherham's three Victoria Cross recipients who lost their lives whilst fighting for our country.

| | |
|---|---|
| GEORGE WILLIAM CHAFER | VC - WW1 |
| THOMAS NORMAN JACKSON | VC - WW1 |
| IAN JOHN McKAY | VC - Falklands War |

Their names are etched around the fountain in the Memorial Garden. The Reverend Canon David Bliss, Vicar of Rotherham, conducted the service that was attended by many people.

The inscription reads –
'In honoured memory of the men of Rotherham awarded the Victoria Cross'

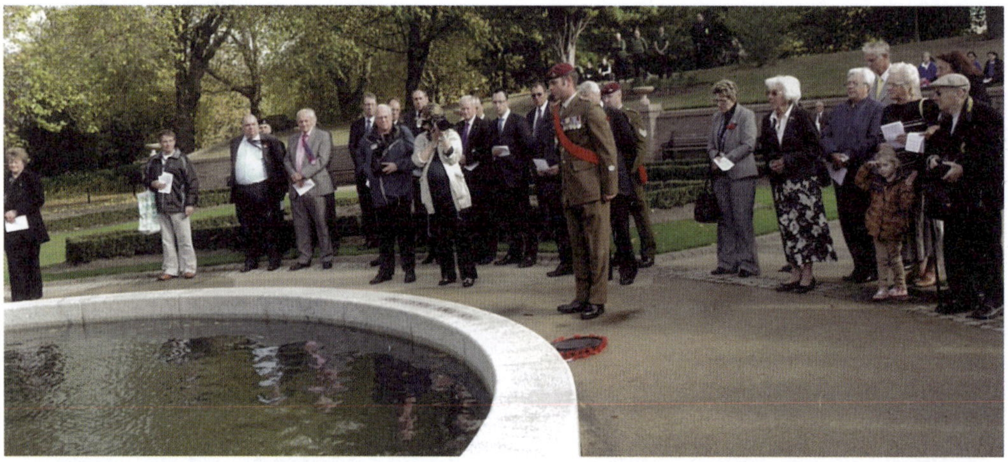

*Simple ceremony at the dedication of the V.C fountain (Author)*

## MEMORIAL ROCK GARDEN

The original rock garden, constructed in the 1950's, has been restored and transformed once again into a beautiful garden. Gentle flowing water runs from the original waterfall, down through the garden into a 'dipping pond'.
The rocks from Ancaster in Lincolnshire weighing between 8 and 17 tons were placed throughout the garden. Timber decking around the pond creates an area for children.

Mrs Ivy Habershon's memorial has been cleaned and replaced and the seating all around make this garden special again. It is a fact that many beautiful wedding photographs have been taken in this garden and other special places around the park.

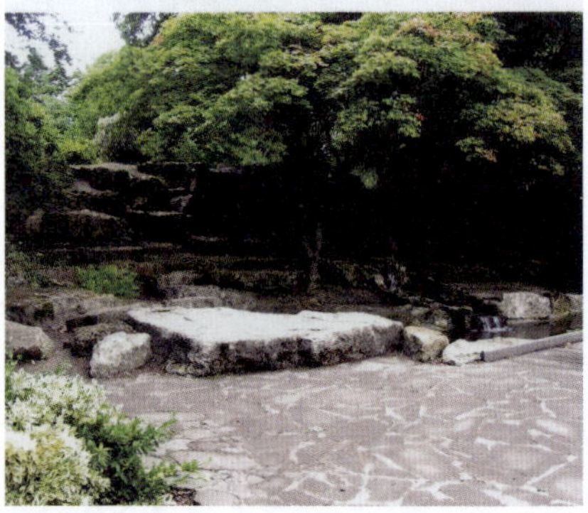

*The rock garden after restoration. (Author)*

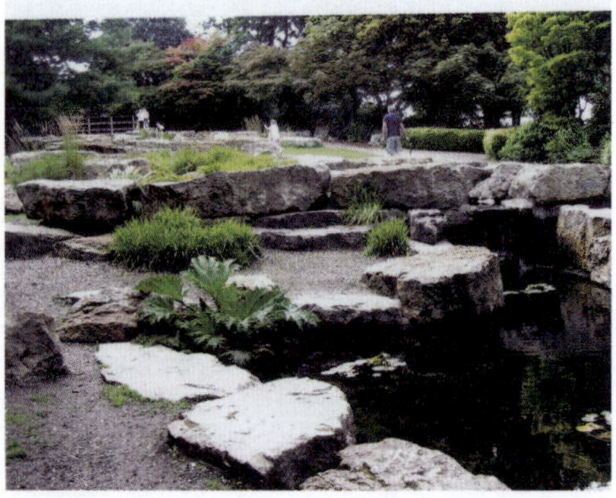

*The dipping pond in the restored rock garden. (Author)*

## BANDSTAND

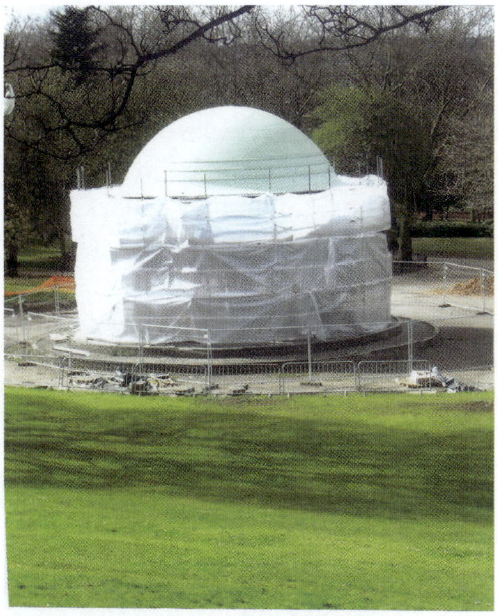

The bandstand under refurbishment. (Author)

The bandstand stands regal after its extensive restoration.

The dome has been repaired and the wood inside the roof replaced as it was completely rotten. New drains and lighting have been installed. Paul Graham, Michael Mather and Tony Rushforth from Clifton Park Museum made the rose in the middle of the ceiling.

The columns have been strengthened and the wooden floor replaced with concrete. (Below the wooden floor was the plinth of the original bandstand which was removed to Masborough Recreational Ground.)

The floor is inscribed with two appropriate sayings:

*'Music is the universal language of mankind.'*
*'If music be the food of love, play on.'*

Sunday afternoon band concerts are once again taking place during the summertime. Various groups of people use it regularly.

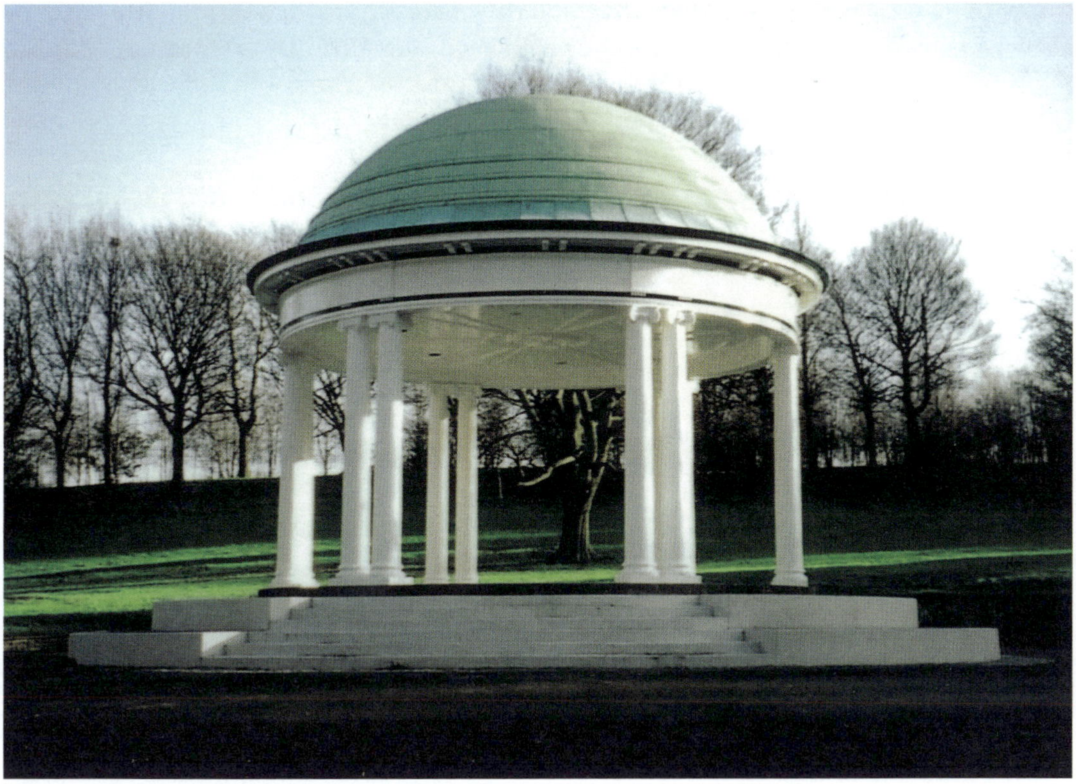

*Refurbished bandstand. (Author)*

## CLIFTON GROVE ENTRANCE

Stone pillars topped with urns were the original ones from the main entrance on Doncaster Road and re-sited to the Clifton Grove entrance in 1900. During the parks restoration they have been moved again, this time to the Museum entrance together with iron gates. The new pillars, replacing the stones ones, are constructed of handmade bricks and match in well with the houses nearby.

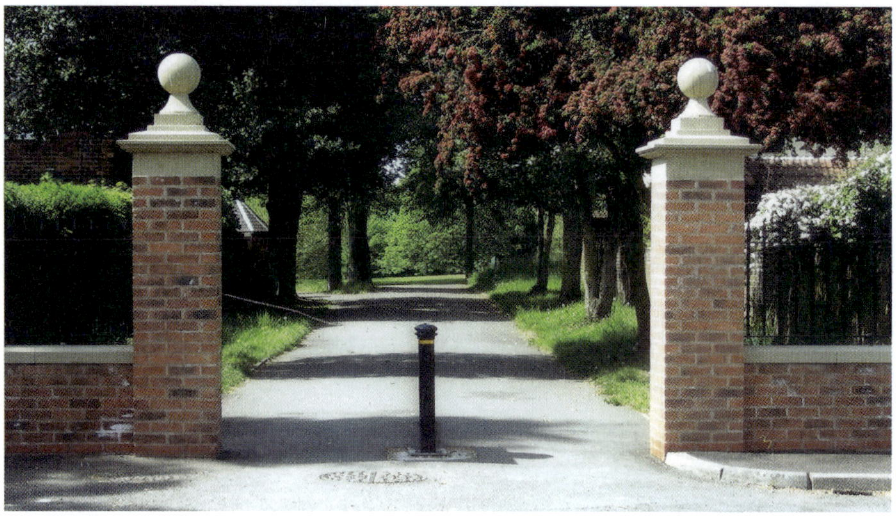

*Hand made brick pillars at Clifton Grove entrance 2010. (Author)*

## WATERPLAY

The old paddling pool has been replaced with a water feature; with fountains, a paddling pool, and whirlpool and water jets that activate at random, it is great fun and people travel from outside of Rotherham to use it. The café is close by so you can enjoy some refreshments and watch the children have the time of their life. There are able and disabled changing facilities so no-one is excluded.

To complement the water play there is the biggest free play park in Yorkshire. 10m tall tower slides, skateboard and BMX park very popular with teenagers, and for younger children there is a huge sand pit to explore! Other play equipment includes tyre swings, a zip wire and entertainment for everyone!

It was officially opened on the 25th July, 2009.

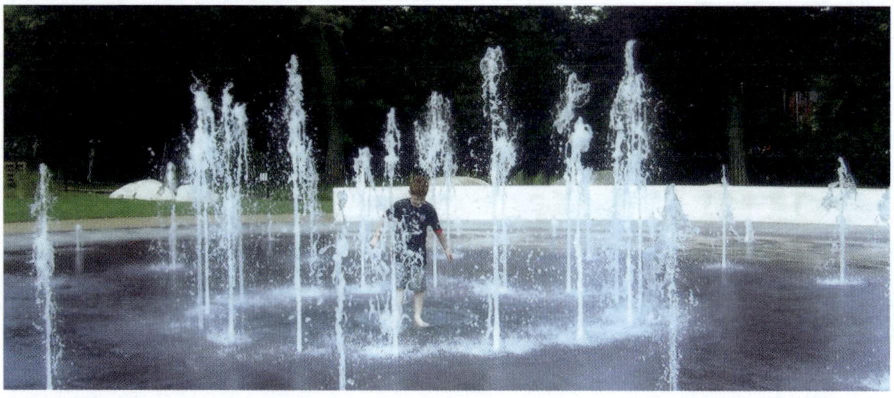

*Ryan testing the new water play, June 2009. (Author)*

## SUNKEN GARDEN

This little used garden has disappeared. In its place a sweeping lawn that Joshua Walker would have seen from his dining room window.

## ROMAN GRANARY

The Rotherham South Area Assembly awarded the Friends of Clifton Park £2,500 to clean and restore the Grade II Listed stones with money from the devolved budget in 2009. This work was completed in the winter of 2010.

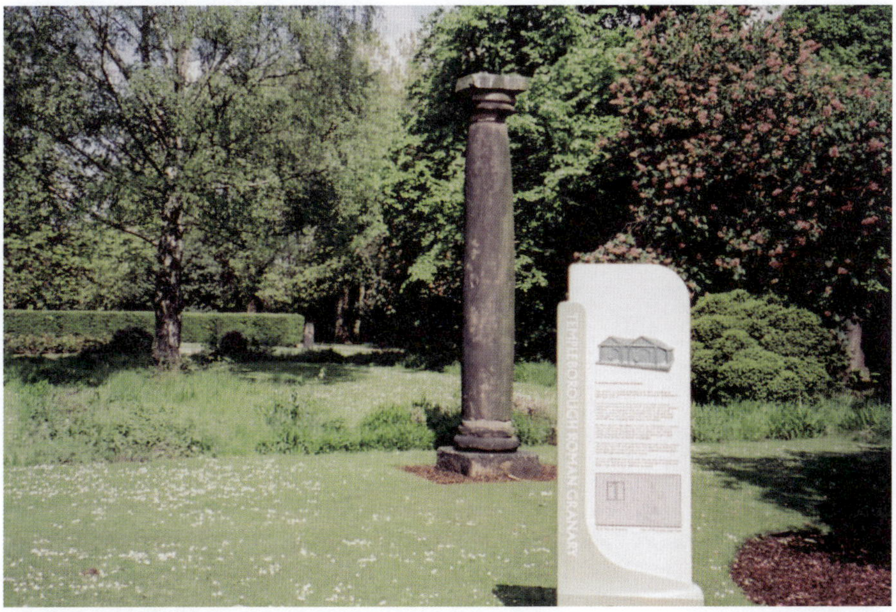

*Roman Granary Monolith. (Author's photograph)*

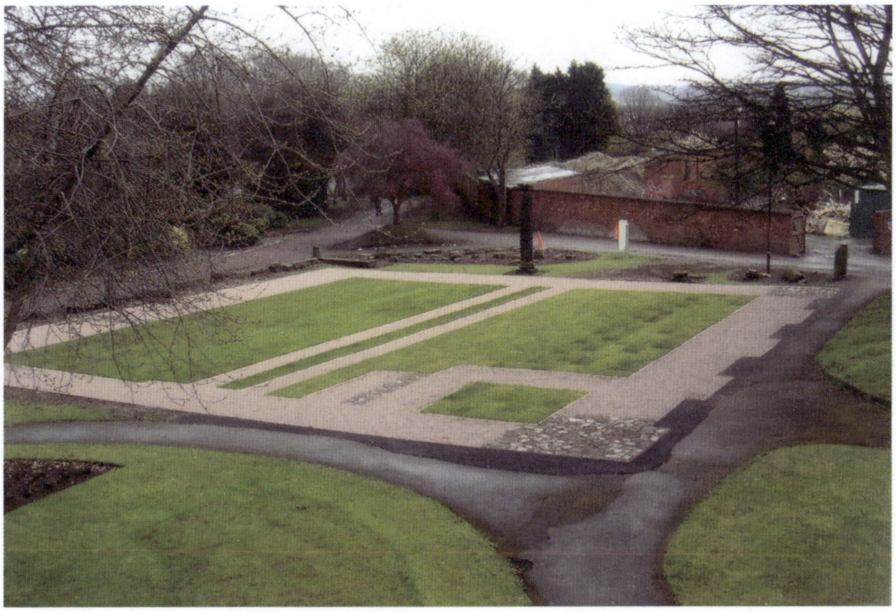

*Roman Granary after restoration, 2008. (Author's photograph)*

## JAY WHEATLEY'S ROUNDABOUTS

18-hole miniature golf course was added in 2009 and the rides were updated.

In the winter of 2010/11, the miniature golf was updated. The 18 hole Golden Putter course fun for all ages, plenty of tricky putts and water hazards to test your skill.

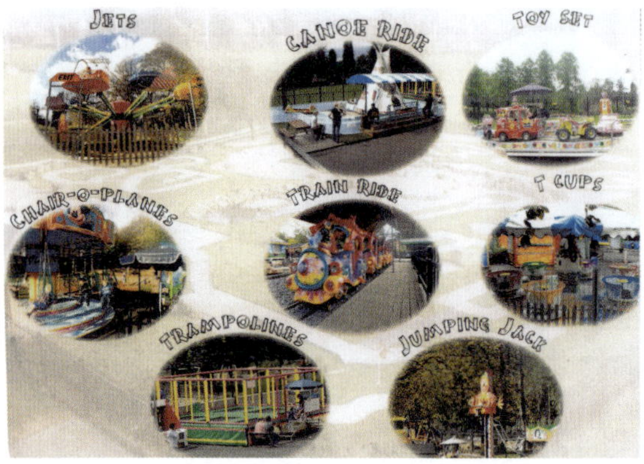


*Jay Wheatley's amusements in Clifton Park 2012. (Jay Wheatley)*

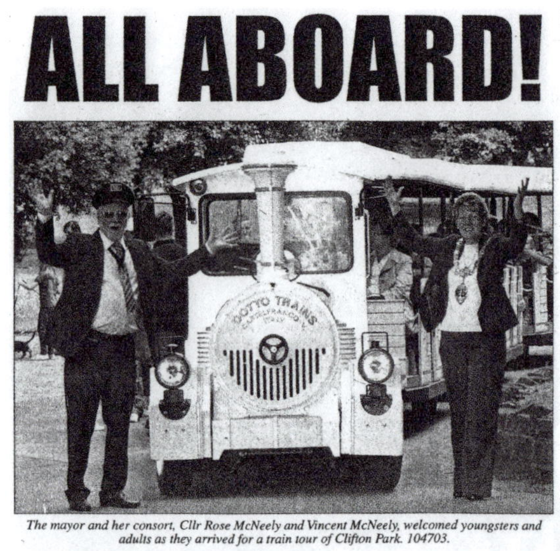

# ALL ABOARD!

The mayor and her consort, Cllr Rose McNeely and Vincent McNeely, welcomed youngsters and adults as they arrived for a train tour of Clifton Park. 104703.

*The train begins it's life in the park, 2010. (Rotherham Advertiser)*

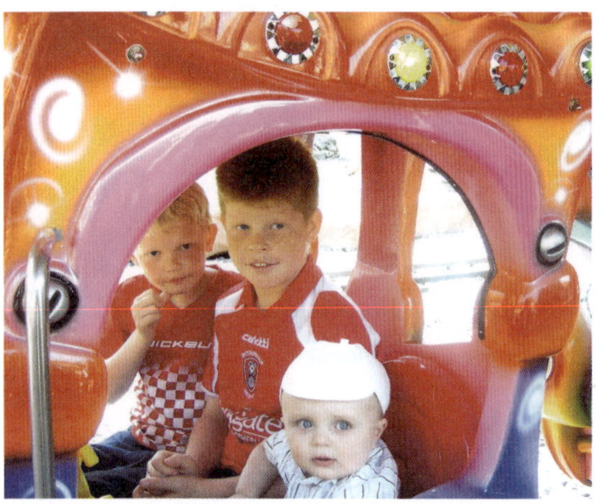

*Jack, Ryan and Jamison riding the train in the funfair, 2010. (Author's photograph)*

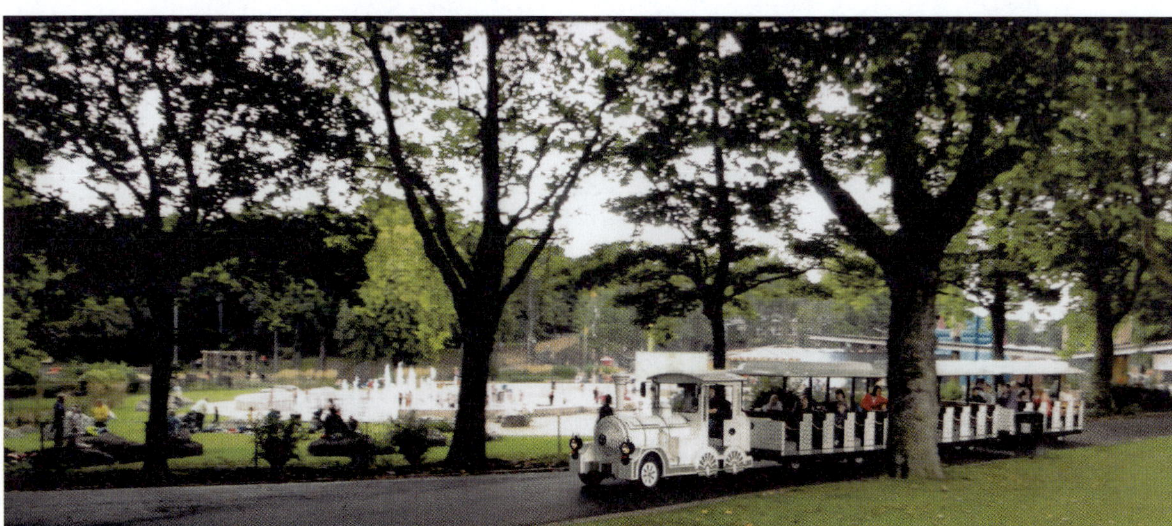

*The train beginning it's journey around the park. (Jay Wheatley)*

## THE GARDEN BUILDING AND COMMUNITY GARDEN

This is the only new build in the park renovation and has been constructed using the latest green technology.

The garden building has a bowling pavilion, multi-function room and ranger accommodation surrounding a courtyard.

Leading from this area is a walled community garden.

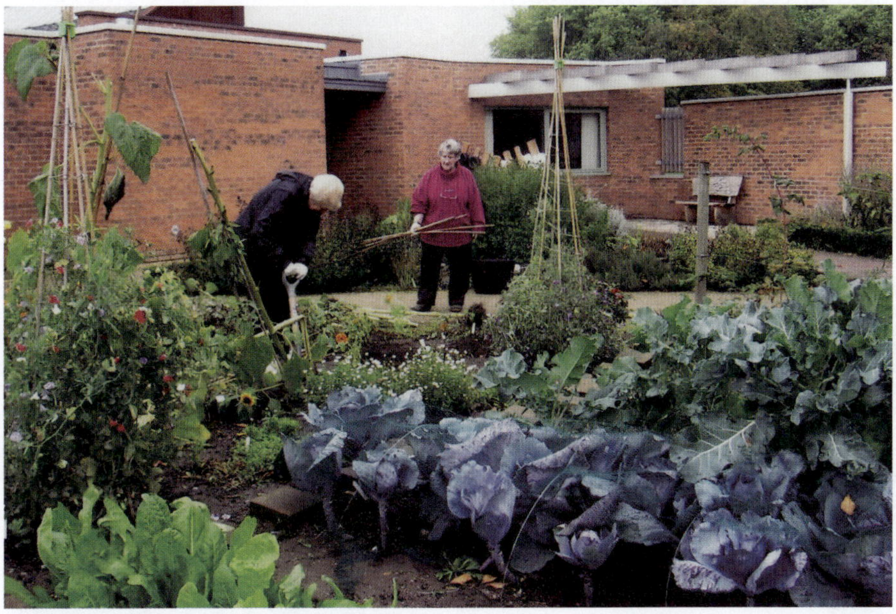

*Volunteers working in the Community Garden, 2012. (Author's photograph)*

The Samuel Walker Sundial stands majestically in this garden and the original trough from the kitchen garden has found a home there. It has been carved from one very large piece of stone most likely during the 18$^{th}$ century.

## FRENCH GARDEN

In November 2010, our twin town St Quentin planted a French Garden near the courtyard of the garden building. The mayor, Councillor Rose McNeely assisted with the planting of this flowerbed. The plants are evergreen with the result of it looking beautiful year-round.

A compass mosaic, designed by the Friends of Clifton Park, is very colourful and can be seen where the pathways cross. It is a durable hand-made pebble mosaic combining modern techniques and imaginative design made by Maggie Howarth, a specialist in this field and based in Lancashire.

The centre of the compass is the Walker Crest, also found on the pottery in the Museum and on their gravestones. In heraldry, the snake or serpent depict wisdom and the dove is loving consistency, peace, and the Holy Spirit. The bees are for efficient industry.

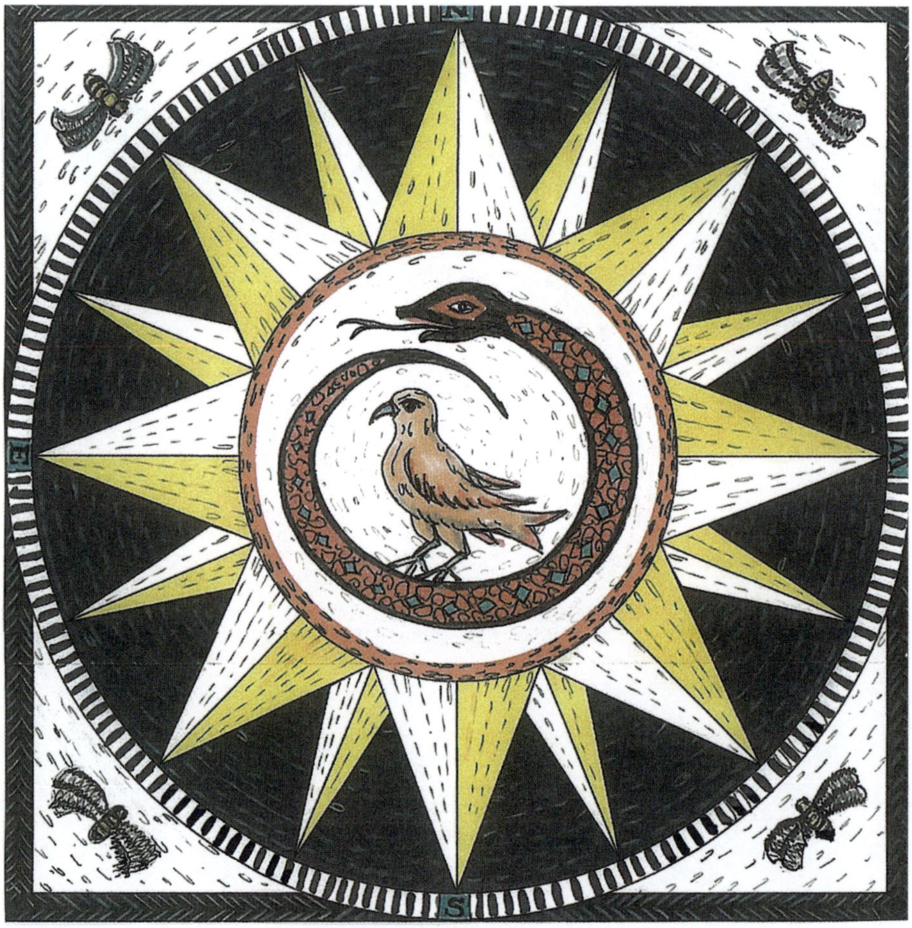

*(Author's photograph)*

## THE WALKER SUNDIAL

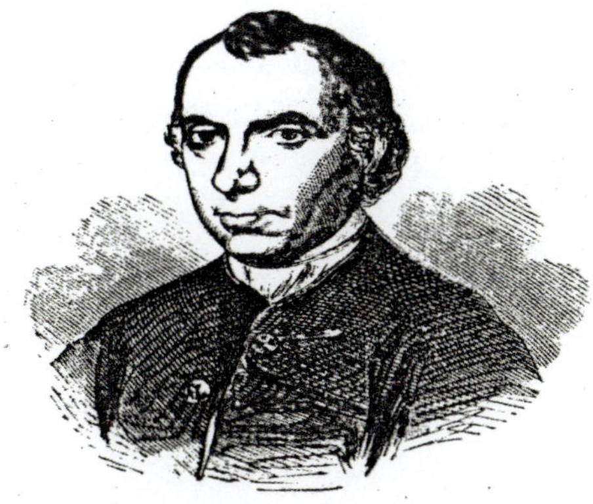

Samuel Walker.

Samuel Walker was the second son of three sons and four daughters and the beginning of the famous Walker family of Rotherham. He was born at Grenoside in November 1715 and orphaned at the age of 12 years. He was self-taught and qualified himself for Grenoside Endowed School until 1746. He taught reading, writing, arithmetic, and the Church Wardens paid him a salary of £1-4 shillings in 1741. He supplemented his living land surveying and making sundials, which were made exactly for each location that they were to be placed. He gave up his profession and joined his brothers Aaron and Jonathon in the 'family business' which began making nails and small iron objects.

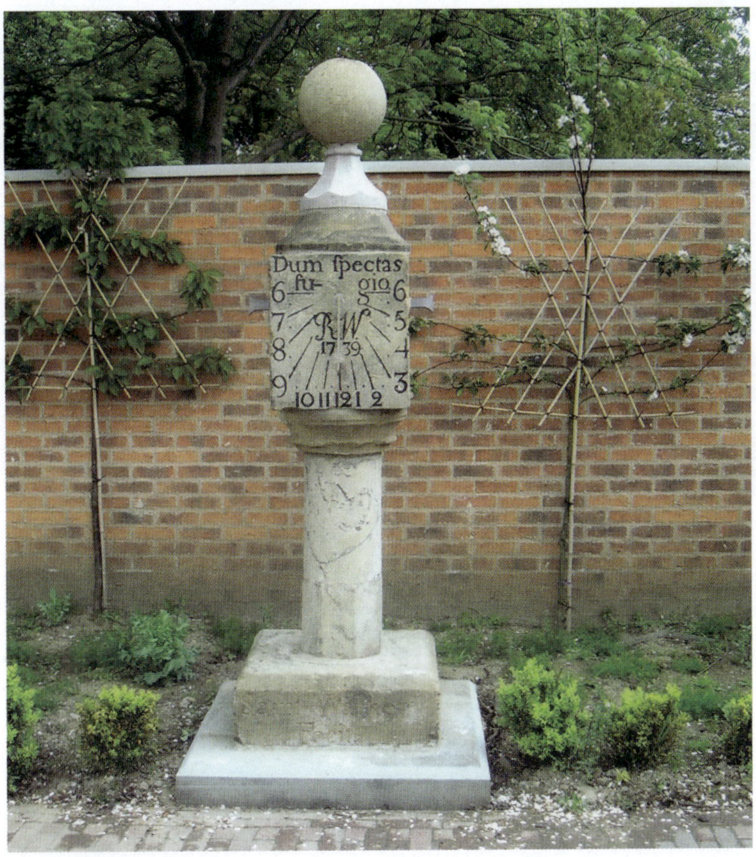


*Samuel Walker Sundial in the Community garden, October 2009. (Author's Photograph)*

He was 23 years old when he made the sundial for Holmes Hall and given the details on the sundial – 17 R.W. 39 – it is tempting to speculate that Samuel made it as a wedding present for his younger brother Aaron who married a Rhoda Wood, daughter of Bartholomew Wood. Rhoda is the only Walker in the family tree to have the initial R, and since they were born in 1718 and 1720 respectively, they would have been the right ages for the date 1739.

The sundial was later moved from Masborough to Ferham House and was in the garden until 1970 when it was moved to the sunken garden in Clifton Park. It cost £150.00 to dismantle, clean and re-erect.

The Sundial was Grade II Listed in 1986.

Dated 17 R.W. 39

Made with ashlar sandstone and chamfered square plinth inscribed:

Sam'l Walker fecit = 'he made it'

Octagonal shaft becoming cylindrical with a cuboid sundial.

Brass gnomons replaced the broken lead gnomons in 2009.

## INSCRIPTIONS:

Dum ipectas fugio = 'I fly away even whilst thou watchest me'
Sic transit Gloria mundi = 'thus passes the glory of the world' / 'thus passes earthly glory'
Juncti valemus = 'being joined we are powerful'

The Sundial was repaired and cleaned and gnomons replaced in 2009 by stone masons working in Clifton Park with donations from sub-contractors.
The stone base which is dated and has the Mason's mark, is reclaimed from stone from the Cenotaph and the ball is resting on a piece of Rotherham red stone, reclaimed from the Memorial Garden.

The Sundial now has a special place in the Community Garden.

## 2012

This was a special year for Clifton Park, Rotherham and the United Kingdom.

In June of that year, Queen Elizabeth II celebrated her Diamond Jubilee.

The Olympic Games were held in London. On its journey from Beijing to London, Rotherham was lucky to have the Olympic Torch in torchbearer mode (actually carried by runners) for the vast majority of the route through the Borough. It was carried through Clifton Park, along the path from the main gates, past the Cenotaph, Bandstand and the children's play area, emerging from the park to re-join the vehicle convoy on Doncaster Road. The park was full of cheering schoolchildren and great crowds of people.

July saw Clifton Park awarded the Green Flag Award. This scheme was set up in 1996 as a benchmark for the national standard for parks and green spaces in the United Kingdom.

On the 6th September the Duke and Duchess of Gloucester officially opened Clifton Park and celebrated the Queens Diamond Jubilee at a Garden Party in the park.

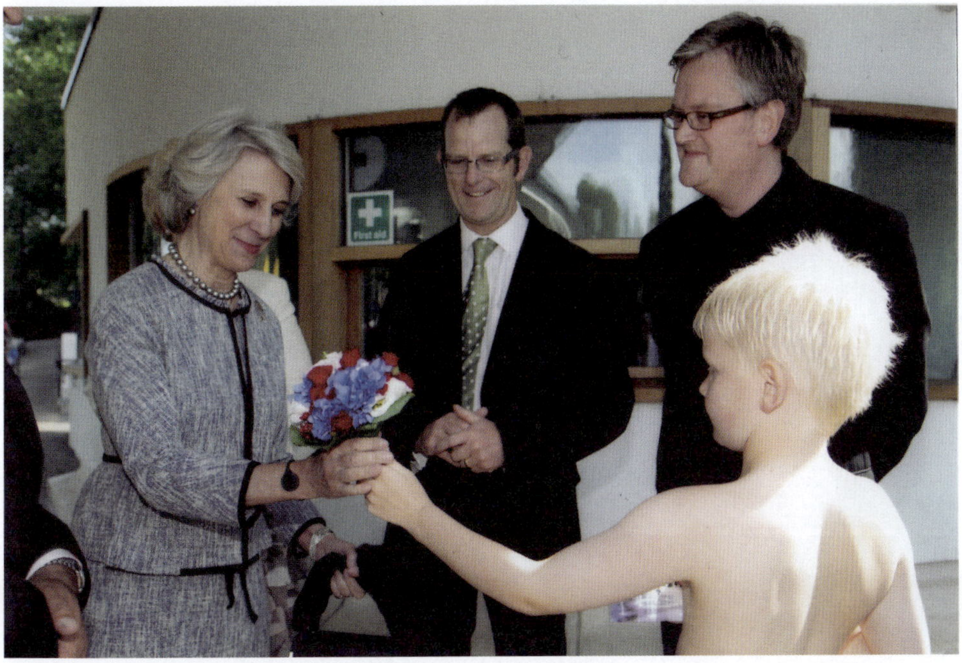

*Restoration of Clifton Park. Jack Green presenting a bouquet to the Duchess of Gloucester, 6th September 2012. (Gerald Humphries)*

In July 2015 Clifton Park was again awarded the Green Flag.
It is the fifth time that it has been named as one of the best parks in the country. The award recognised the work which is carried out by the park staff and volunteers.

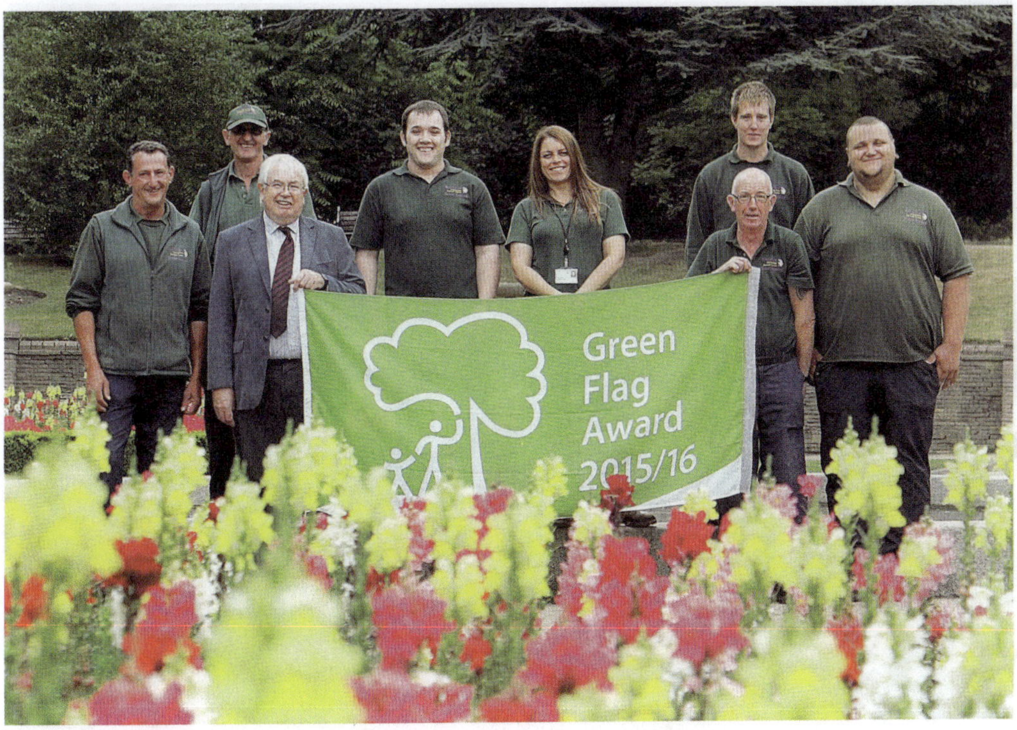


*From left: Gary Larkin, Glenn Foord, CLLR David Roche, Adam Holmes, Andrea Jones, Simon Carr, Keith Burns and James Taylor. (Andy Lee)*

## 35 WORLD WAR II MEMORIAL

A place was set aside in the memorial garden during the park restoration for a memorial to be erected to honour the men and women of Rotherham who died during World War II.

The Friends of Clifton Park began raising money in 2008 and reached their goal in 2015. Donations from the people of Rotherham, businesses, local councillors, regiments, veterans, raffles and auctions to name a few raised £32,500.00.

Talks were held and Mr Steve Davies of Davies Stone Mason's of Bawtry made a beautiful memorial. It is made of York stone with black Granite inserts. The centre piece has the dedication and ten others contain 1,126 names of the fallen who lived in Rotherham Metropolitan Borough as it is today.

On the 16th September 2015 at 10am on a cool autumnal morning a simple, moving dedication ceremony was held lead by Canon David Bliss assisted by Rev. Abbi Thompson, Vicar of Clifton.

Wreaths were laid by the Lord Lieutenant of South Yorkshire Mr. Andrew J. Coombe, the Mayor of Rotherham Councillor Maggi Clarke, The Friends of Clifton Park, The Fellowship of the Services and the relatives of the fallen.

Many people attended the ceremony which will be remembered for many years and the memorial garden will provide a place of quiet reflection of the times past.

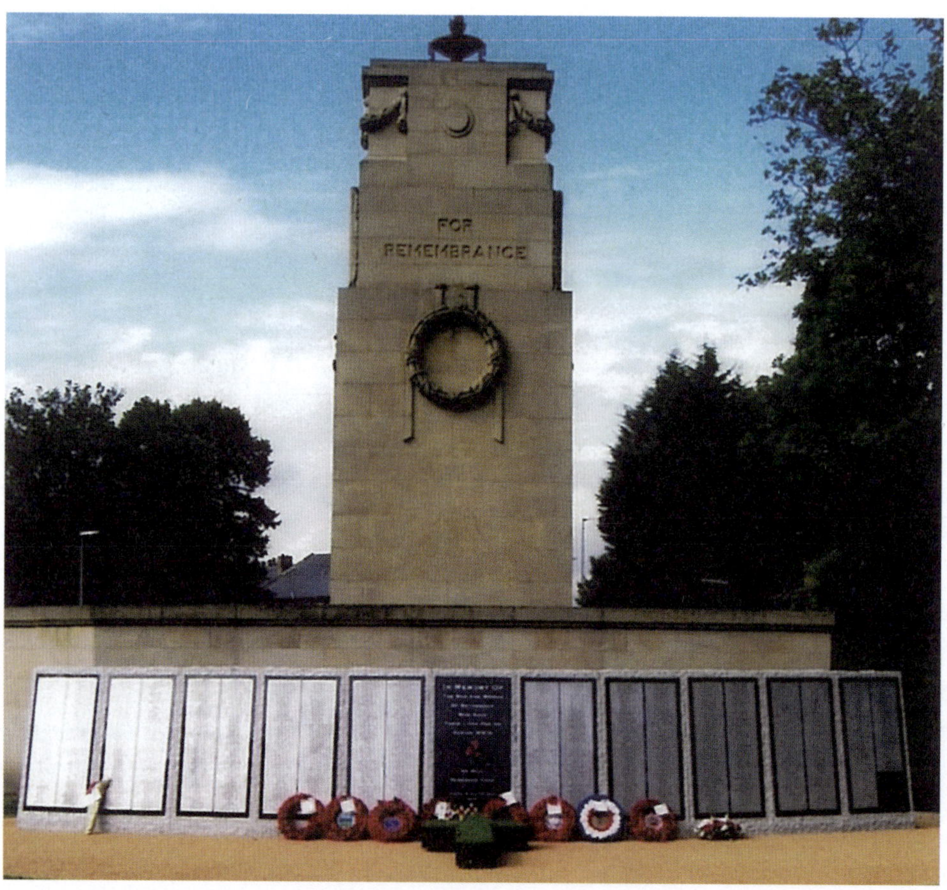

## *A Special Place*

*Take my hand and come with me*
*To a special place across the sea*
*A sacred place in hallowed ground*
*A place where love and sorrow are found*
*It's not a church you understand*
*Just part of home in another land*
*A place where gravestones stand arrayed*
*Like phantom army on parade*
*Stand close to me and patience keep*
*And soon you'll see a brave man weep*
*He cries for his comrade beneath the stone*
*And tells your friend he's not alone*
*Scenes like this are common place*
*So as you stroll down memory lane*
*Think of them who must remain*
*But now they're home, but just in name*
*And now its time to say "Adieu"*
*But remember friends they died for you.*

*Poem recited at the end of the service by Rev. Abbi Thompson*

To quote an article written in the Rotherham Advertiser in 1949

*People passing through Rotherham on the train, or, indeed by car get a very poor impression of the town.*
*Railway passengers catch very little but a panorama of factory chimneys belching smoke, of squalid houses with little or no garden to speak of; a complete absence of green fields. So they pass through to the talk of Rotherham as a town of dirt and grime, with nothing in the way of beauty.*

I wonder what those same people would say now if they could see all our garden spaces especially Clifton Park?

## BIBLIOGRAPHY


| | |
|---|---|
| Rotherham | Freda Crowder and Dorothy Green |
| Memory Lane, Rotherham | John Tunny |
| Rotherham As It Was | Robert G. Neville and John Benson |
| Rotherham, a Pictorial History | Anthony P. Munford |
| Rotherham 1945: a Time to Remember | R.M.B.C. Department of Libraries, Museum & Arts |
| www.rotherham.co.uk | Sunshine Corner Memories |
| Rotherham Then & Now | Freda Crowder & Alan Turner |

Rotherham Borough Centenary Celebrations 1971

A History of Rotherham — Anthony P. Munford

The Royal Story, programme of Royal events, Rotherham 1953

Rotherham Directory 1902

Clifton House and Park — R.M.B.C. Department of Libraries, Museum and Arts

www.rotherweb.co.uk/memories.shirley

The Building Stones of Rotherham: a geographical guide by Michael Clarke

Round and about Grenoside Vol. 4, our village story — Chris Morley

Rotherham Advertiser – various editions from 1891 to present day

Archives & Local Studies section, Central Library and Arts Centre

Clifton Park Museum, Rotherham. Report on the History of the Gardens and Parkland of Clifton House — Jane Firse, November 2003

Council Recreation Committee minutes

Rotherham Then and Now — Margaret and Chris Drinkall

Rotherham Annuals